The Shakespeare Handbooks
Shakespeare's Contemporaries

John Webster
The Duchess of Malfi

David Carnegie

D1391096

palgrave
macmillan

First published 2014 by
PALGRAVE MACMILLAN

Palgrave Macmillan in the UK is an imprint of Macmillan Publishers Limited, registered in England, company number 785998, of Houndmills, Basingstoke, Hampshire RG21 6XS.

Palgrave Macmillan in the US is a division of St Martin's Press LLC, 175 Fifth Avenue, New York, NY 10010.

Palgrave Macmillan is the global academic imprint of the above companies and has companies and representatives throughout the world.

Palgrave® and Macmillan® are registered trademarks in the United States, the United Kingdom, Europe and other countries

ISBN: 978–0–230–24374–3 hardback
ISBN: 978–0–230–24375–0 paperback

This book is printed on paper suitable for recycling and made from fully managed and sustained forest sources. Logging, pulping and manufacturing processes are expected to conform to the environmental regulations of the country of origin.

A catalogue record for this book is available from the British Library.

A catalog record for this book is available from the Library of Congress.

Printed in China

Contents

Series Editors' Preface

The Shakespeare Handbooks provide an innovative way of studying the plays of Shakespeare and his contemporaries in performance. The commentaries, which are their core feature, enable a reader to envisage the words of a text unfurling in performance, involving actions and meanings not readily perceived except in rehearsal or performance. The aim is to present the plays in the environment for which they were written and to offer an experience as close as possible to an audience's progressive experience of a production.

While each book has the same range of contents, their authors have been encouraged to shape them according to their own critical and scholarly understanding and their first-hand experience of theatre practice. The various chapters are designed to complement the commentaries: the cultural context of each play is presented together with quotations from original sources; the authority of its text or texts is considered with what is known of the earliest performances; key performances and productions of its subsequent stage history are both described and compared; an account is given of influential criticism of the play and the more significant is quoted extensively. The aim in all this has been to help readers to develop their own informed and imaginative view of a play in ways that supplement the provision of standard editions and are more user-friendly than detailed stage histories or collections of criticism from diverse sources.

We would like to acknowledge a special debt of gratitude to the founder of the Shakespeare Handbooks Series, John Russell Brown, whose energy for life, literature and theatre we continue to find truly inspiring.

Paul Edmondson and Kevin Ewert

Preface

It is a joy to attend a performance of *The Duchess of Malfi*, one of the finest tragedies of what we often call the Shakespearean period, not least because we have relatively few opportunities to see the plays of John Webster and others compared to the many productions of Shakespeare.

To write about a Webster play is to relive earlier productions, but it is also to call on every available resource of both scholarship and the theatre. I am indebted to all the writers whom I quote, and many more besides, whose research has helped form such knowledge, critical thinking, and judgement as I can claim. In addition, I am grateful to the many actors, directors, designers, technicians, and dramaturgs whom I have worked with and learned from. Bringing together the all-too-often-separate worlds of the university and the working theatre is productive indeed.

It is a pleasure to acknowledge a few more specific debts. First, to the founding general editor of this series, and outstanding Webster scholar, John Russell Brown. From my colleagues and friends David Gunby and the late Antony Hammond, co-editors of *The Duchess of Malfi* for the Cambridge *Works of John Webster*, I received support and encouragement in my then-radical determination to pay full attention to Webster's stagecraft and performance as well as to literary criticism. From both of them, and from Mac Jackson, I have learned much. I benefited greatly from my first outing as a professional dramaturg, for Colin McColl's 1982 production of the play for Circa Theatre in Wellington. In 2010 I enjoyed the hospitality of Jesse Berger's Red Bull Theater in New York, and I was disappointed not to be able to include Jesse's *Duchess of Malfi* as one of the productions for detailed analysis. To Pascale Aebischer I owe thanks for a pre-publication copy of her chapter 'Early Modern Performance and Digital Media: Remediation and the Evolving Archival Canon', in *Beyond Shakespeare: Screening*

Early Modern Drama (Cambridge: Cambridge University Press, 2013), as to Rowland Wymer and Palgrave Macmillan for access to a pre-publication copy of his article 'The Duchess of Malfi on Film: Peter Huby's Quietus', in *Reinventing the Renaissance: Shakespeare and his Contemporaries in Adaptation and Performance*, ed. Sarah Brown, Robert Lublin, and Lynsey McCulloch (Basingstoke: Palgrave Macmillan, 2013). I thank David Lawrence for research assistance both on early texts and on film and audio versions of the play. And to my university and theatre colleagues, and to all my students who explored Webster in productions and workshops, I offer deep appreciation. I also owe a debt to Victoria University of Wellington for academic leave, research funding, library resources, and much more.

Among many libraries and theatre archives I owe special thanks to the Billy Rose Theatre Collection at the New York Public Library, the Folger Shakespeare Library, the Huntington Library, the National Theatre in London, the Shakespeare Centre in Stratford-upon-Avon, and the Victoria and Albert Museum's theatre archive. I am desperately sorry not to have seen Dominic Dromgoole's production of *The Duchess of Malfi* in the new Sam Wanamaker Theatre at Shakespeare's Globe in London, performed by candlelight in a building very similar to that for which the play was originally written; and I am equally sorry it was too late for inclusion in this book. Thanks also to all the theatre critics whose records of performances are so vital to a work like this. In addition, Sonya Barker, Felicity Noble, and all the other staff at Palgrave Macmillan have been unfailingly supportive. Paul Edmondson has been an admirable general editor, and Alec McAulay a vigilant copy-editor.

A final thank you must go to Gisella Carr for unwavering love and faith.

1 The Text and Early Performances

I will entertain you with what hath happened this week at the bank's side. The King's players had a new play, called All is True, *representing some principal pieces of the reign of Henry VIII, which was set forth with many extraordinary circumstances of pomp and majesty, even to the matting of the stage; the Knights of the Order, with their Georges and Garters, the guards, with their embroidered coats, and the like: sufficient in truth within a while to make greatness very familiar, if not ridiculous. Now, King Henry making a masque at the Cardinal Wolsey's house, and certain chambers being shot off at his entry, some of the paper, or other stuff, wherewith one of them was stopped, did light on the thatch, where being thought at first but an idle smoke, and their eyes more attentive to the show, it kindled inwardly, and ran round like a train, consuming within less than an hour the whole house to the very grounds.*

This was the fatal period of that virtuous fabric; wherein yet nothing did perish but wood and straw, and a few forsaken cloaks; only one man had his breeches set on fire, that would perhaps have broiled him, if he had not by the benefit of a provident wit put it out with bottle ale.

(Fire at the Globe Theatre, 29 June 1613;
letter from Sir Henry Wotton)

THE TRAGEDY OF THE DUCHESS OF MALFI.

As it was presented privately, at the Blackfriars; and publicly at the Globe, by the King's Majesty's Servants.

The perfect and exact copy, with divers things printed that the length of the play would not bear in the presentment.

(Title page, Quarto 1, 1623)

The two extracts printed above have much to say about the theatrical conditions of composition, performance, and publication for both John Fletcher and William Shakespeare's *All is True* (better known as *King Henry VIII*), and for John Webster's *The Duchess of Malfi*.

Most immediately, the fire that razed the outdoor 'public' first Globe theatre to the ground in June 1613 meant that the King's Men, the theatre company in which Shakespeare had acted until about this time, and for whom he had written most of his plays, had to adapt rapidly to performing only in their much smaller, elite, indoor, 'private' theatre, the Blackfriars. The rebuilt theatre, the second Globe, would take a year to complete, so in the meantime the King's Men may well have been looking for playwrights to provide new plays suited to the somewhat different conditions of the Blackfriars (akin to the new Sam Wannamaker Playhouse at Shakespeare's Globe in London, a reconstruction based on seventeenth-century plans for an indoor playhouse; it opened in 2014 with a production of *The Duchess of Malfi*, a fitting quatercentennial memorial).

John Webster would have been a likely candidate, as he was a playwright with experience of writing for the private theatres. He had collaborated with Thomas Dekker about ten years earlier on two plays for the Children of Paul's, the boy company playing in a small indoor theatre in the precincts of St Paul's Cathedral. He had also worked for the King's Men about the same time, revising a boy company play called *The Malcontent*, by John Marston, for performance by the adult actors at the 'public' first Globe in 1604. The revision included an Induction for which he wrote parts specifically for the leading actors in the company: Richard Burbage, Henry Condell, John Lowin, and Will Sly. As we shall see, the first three of these were still in the company, and we know which roles Webster wrote for them when they performed *The Duchess of Malfi* in late 1613 or 1614. And only the year before the Globe fire Webster had complained in the published edition of his tragedy *The White Devil*, a major play also set in Italy, about the 'ignorant asses' who comprised his audience at the down-market Red Bull playhouse. His carefully and densely constructed plays required the sort of educated audience to be found in the expensive private playhouses.

We know that Webster was already writing *The Duchess of Malfi* in 1612, but that he did not finish it until well into 1613, or possibly as late as 1614, but we also know that William Ostler, one of the actors, died in late 1614 (see below), so the play was certainly being performed before then, probably first '*privately, at the Blackfriars*' and only later '*publicly at the Globe*', following the rebuilding after the fire.

We are fortunate to have several eyewitness reactions to those early performances. Commendatory verses by his fellow playwrights Thomas Middleton and William Rowley for the 1623 publication of the play are, as was required on such occasions, uncritically flattering. Nevertheless, it is instructive to note that Middleton focuses on the centrality of the Duchess, and the pathos of her death:

> Write, 'Duchess', that will fetch a tear for thee.
> For whoe'er saw this duchess live and die,
> That could get off under a bleeding eye?
>
> (16–18)

He is responding to performance: whoever '*saw* this duchess' was moved to tears. Rowley's attention is also on the Duchess 'lively bodied in thy play' (i.e., embodied, enacted), especially her speech in defence of Antonio, 'her low-rated love', against 'Her brothers' anger' (27–8). For Rowley, Antonio's low birth was sufficient explanation for the fatal revenge of the Aragonian brothers, and the Duchess's speeches in Antonio's defence impressive in performance.

A third eyewitness was less impressed. Orazio Busino, chaplain to the Venetian embassy in London, was citing the performance in order to report and complain to his masters in Venice how English antagonism to Roman Catholicism carried even into stage representation (see pp. 91–2). For our purposes here, and even allowing for his confusions and mistakes about the play, his recollection of the erection of an altar on stage, the impression made by costume in the transformation of the Cardinal from churchman to warrior, and his appearance 'in public with a harlot on his knee' give us useful evidence about specifics he presumably saw at the Blackfriars or Globe.

If it was at the Blackfriars, the private theatre practice of entr'acte music would have reinforced the neoclassical five-act structure of *The Duchess of Malfi* in which plot time elapses between each act. The play avoids large 'trumpets and drums' battle scenes that were so popular with the public theatre audiences, and the surviving music for the Madmen's song seems intended for the indoor acoustic of the smaller private theatres. The fact that the private theatres, holding only about a sixth the number of audience members as the public theatres, charged up to six times as much for admission guaranteed a wealthy and educated audience such as Webster sought.

Nevertheless, we need to recall the play was also acted '*publicly at the Globe*'. Like most of the company's plays at this period, it could be and was performed in both spaces. The theatres were alike, we think, in relying on an open platform stage on which the actors and their costumes and props, not scenery, provided the main spectacle. On a stage with certainly two doors, one at each end of the tiring-house facade behind the actors, and probably a central opening for spectacular entries, the choice of door could be significant for meaning. In Act I of *The Duchess of Malfi* Antonio and Delio observe the successive entrances of Bosola; the Cardinal; Silvio, Castruchio, Julia, Roderigo, and Grisolan; Duke Ferdinand; and then the Cardinal again, with the Duchess, Cariola, and Attendants. If they all enter from the same door, this reinforces Delio's comment that 'The presence [chamber] 'gins to fill' (I.i.82). In other words, everybody is coming in by the same door to the Duchess's presence chamber, or throne room, and the order of their arrival is the only emphasis: the Duchess arrives last, once everyone else is assembled. However, if everyone else arrives by one (or even both) of the doors to the side, and the Duchess and her entourage arrive by the more ceremonial central entry, her position as presiding in her own presence-chamber is strongly reinforced, especially if all her courtiers kneel to her, and even more so if there is a 'state', a dais with a canopied throne upon it, to which she ascends.

The identification of doors must be different by the end of the act, though, since we would not for a moment imagine that the private, secret wooing scene for which the Duchess has sent for Antonio takes place in the public presence chamber. Once we do not need a specific location, the doors, and indeed the space itself, can become neutral, only to become specific again as needed. When Antonio tells Bosola 'this door you pass not: / I do not hold it fit that you come near / The Duchess' lodgings' (II.iii.48–50), we understand that 'this door' in the palace allows access to the 'Duchess' lodgings'. Sometimes, however, they are merely the theatre's doors, not part of the fiction at all. When Ferdinand in Rome in III.iii sends Bosola away to get soldiers, the two men probably exit by different doors to indicate going in different directions. But the next moment two Pilgrims enter at Loretto through one of the same two doors; they have simply entered onto the stage and announced they are in front of the shrine. The doors are merely functional this time, though dramatically charged elsewhere. The dramaturgy is powerful because so simple and so fluid.

Covering the central opening, and perhaps even all the doors, were hangings or curtains: 'place thyself behind the arras' is the Duchess's instruction to Cariola at I.i.357, using the arras as a place for secret listening, as do the King and Polonius in *Hamlet*. The arras was probably drawn aside to 'discover' (uncover, reveal) the waxworks in IV.i, and perhaps again to reveal the dead children in IV.ii. At a level higher than the doors and the main stage was an upper acting area known as the gallery or terrace (or because of *Romeo and Juliet*, often now as the balcony). Webster brings this into play in Act V when Pescara tells the audience he will descend (backstage) to assist the Cardinal; this makes visual sense of Bosola killing Antonio's servant so that he cannot 'unbarricade the door / To let in rescue' (V.v.35–6).

Equally important on a bare stage is costume, as Wotton's letter about *All is True* makes clear, especially the rich costumes of nobility and royalty. *The Duchess of Malfi* deploys visual codes of clothing to which the Jacobean audience was thoroughly attuned. Antonio, an Italian in Italy, appears in the first scene 'A very formal Frenchman in your habit' (I.i.3), an outsider in the cut of his clothes and the steward's chain he wears about his neck. Bosola, another outsider in the play, may wear black throughout, to indicate his nature as a malcontent. The Duchess herself hides her pregnancy by wearing 'a loose-bodied gown', described by Bosola to the audience as 'contrary to our Italian fashion' (II.i.70–71).

Profession, social standing, and wealth are usually signalled by costume: the Cardinal's robes (and subsequent '*sword, helmet, shield, and spurs*' [III.iv.7.3–.4'], and 'soldier's sash' seen by Busino), the leather jerkins of the soldiers, the recognizable attire of pilgrims (in long gowns, carrying a walking staff, and wearing the distinctive scallop shell of pilgrimage), Castruchio's probable lawyer's gown and coif, the plain woollen clothing of servants alongside the extravagant silk,

---

1 Decimal points following a line number indicate a stage direction following that line. Thus 'III.iv.7.3–.4' signals the third and fourth lines of a stage direction following line 7.

velvet, and jewels of Ferdinand and the Duchess, all will place the characters immediately in a recognizable context. Departures and arrivals from Malfi, Rome, Milan, and Ancona will be visually evident from cloaks and spurs worn by the men, and 'safeguards' worn by the women to protect their dresses when riding.

Even hair and masks are important: Ferdinand comments on the Doctor's possibly comic eyebrows and beard, while the soldiers who capture the Duchess are vizarded (masked). Ferdinand had warned the Duchess earlier that 'A visor and a mask' are not employed 'for goodness' (I.i.334–5), and the masque (two versions of the same word) of Madmen reinforces the point. Bosola enters *as an old man* at IV.ii.113.2, and describes himself sequentially as a tomb-maker, a bellman, an executor, a confessor, and an executioner; no doubt in long robes, probably cowled, he appears symbolic, the traditional figure of Time or Death.

Large properties, such as the 'state' discussed earlier, or the altar erected for the Cardinal at Loretto are also important. In this play they are particularly spectacular, including the elaborate, apparently waxwork, effigies of the dead Antonio and his children, and the tomb in V.iii. Antonio, as he listens to the final echo of the Duchess, tells Delio, 'on the sudden, a clear light / Presented me a face folded in sorrow' (V.iii.44–5). It is possible Webster asked for the same tomb he would have seen the King's Men use in Middleton's *The Lady's Tragedy* (aka *The Second Maiden's Tragedy*) in 1611, in which *'the tombstone flies open, and a great light appears in the midst of the tomb; his Lady, as went out, standing just before him all in white'* (IV.iv.42.2–.5). We cannot be sure, but the possibility would fit with Webster's dramaturgy, in which visual spectacle plays an essential role in telling the story.

Small props, often symbolic as much as functional, similarly help orient the audience in its reception of the play's emotion and meaning. As in, for example, *Hamlet* or *Julius Caesar*, a book such as the Cardinal carries when he enters in the final scene signals melancholy; then Webster intensifies the characterization by telling us the content. Antonio sees within the Duchess's wedding ring 'a sawcy and ambitious devil' (I.i.412), and the Duchess's mirror reflects her signs of age, and even an instrument of death. Her marriage and death are jointly celebrated with gifts of coffin, bell, and strangling cords on stage.

Some props are conventional rather than functional, such as torches and Bosola's dark lantern: audience and actors shared the available light at both the Blackfriars (candle-lit) and the Globe (daylight), so actors brought lights on stage not to increase the real illumination in the theatre, but to signal darkness in the fictional story, in the drama. This is especially important in considering the dead hand sequence in IV.i; it is very likely Webster intended the audience to recognize Ferdinand's trick before the Duchess does. She displays sudden shock and horror at the discovery, but the audience has had time to absorb what is happening, and to think about the implications. Such is Webster's dramatic method.

The playwright also had to structure the play so that the company's usual complement of ten or so principal actors, six or so 'hired men' playing minor roles, and as many boys as needed to play women and children, could manage to play substantially more characters than they had actors; in other words, to double. We assume that the actors of such major roles as Bosola, Ferdinand, the Cardinal, and Antonio did not double, nor the boy actors playing the Duchess, Cariola, and Julia, but a list of actors and roles in the first edition of the play (see below) informs us that the actor of Delio doubled as a Madman, and we can assume that Rodorigo, Grisolan, and one other also doubled as Madmen.

Further investigation of casting and doubling suggests the likelihood that since Castruchio is written out after II.i, he may also have played Malateste and a Madman. With this in mind, we may compare the comedy of Castruchio and the figure of fun Malateste. Silvio disappears from the play after III.iii, cannot double either Malateste or Pescara (since they are also in III.iii), but would have been available to play the Doctor in V.ii. There were probably ten or so principal actors, with four to six 'hired men' playing the four Servants and Officers in II.ii and III.ii, as well as Churchmen in III.iv, Guards in III.v, extra Madmen and the Executioners in IV.ii, in addition to various other servants and attendants.

The seven roles for women and boys may have had individual boy actors, although that number could easily be reduced to six by having the Old Lady double as the 'tedious lady' of II.i, or even to five by having the actors of the two older children also playing both these ladies. But boys do not seem to have been in short supply for the stage.

The earliest publication of the play, in 1623, includes a remarkable list of 'The Actors' Names', the first-ever such list in English to assign actors to specific roles. As a result, we know who played most of the main roles, including instances of cast changes between the original performances and post-1619 performances. The role with the most lines, that of Bosola, was played by John Lowin. By 1614 he was an established core actor approaching 40 who had been with the company more than ten years. He is thought to have specialized in bluff outspoken roles such as Falstaff and Henry VIII, so was probably a large man. In the early performances Ferdinand and his brother the Cardinal were played by Richard Burbage and Henry Condell (the latter would be co-editor of the Shakespeare First Folio in 1623), both veterans of the company. Burbage was part of the founding family, and the leading actor from about 1592 to his death in 1619. Shakespeare wrote many parts for him, including Hamlet, Lear, Othello – and Richard III. When Ferdinand in *The Duchess of Malfi*, played by Burbage, enters in the final scene in the belief he is in the middle of a battle, and cries, 'Give me a fresh horse' (V.v.47), many in the audience presumably recognized the self-consciously theatrical (metatheatrical) grotesquerie of the echo from *Richard III* ('A horse! A horse! My kingdom for a horse!' [V.vii.7]) declaimed by the same actor. Two younger men played Antonio and Delio: William Ostler, probably in his mid twenties in 1614, and his contemporary John Underwood.

Ostler died in December 1614, Burbage in March 1619, and Condell retired in 1619. In fact, there was considerable turnover in the company by 1623, and a number of younger actors evidently took over the roles of dead or retired actors after 1619. Whereas in the first presentations of *The Duchess of Malfi* Bosola, Ferdinand, and the Cardinal were played by a middle-aged trio of leading actors facing younger actors as Antonio and Delio, by 1623 Lowin's Bosola was ten years older than the new actor of Ferdinand and 20 years older than the Cardinal (the young Richard Robinson, who probably played the Duchess in the early performances). We cannot know how significant such age differences were in Jacobean acting (Burbage was playing the young Hamlet at the same time as the aged King Lear), but certainly Lowin must have been a commanding figure as Bosola by 1623.

The first quarto text of
The Duchess of Malfi, 1623

The first actors of *The Tragedy of the Dutchesse of Malfy* (as it is called in the first published edition, a quarto of 1623, referred to hereafter as Q1) did not have a printed book from which to learn their parts or study the play; they had only handwritten copies of their own parts, with the skimpiest of cues indicating when to speak. There would have been a complete manuscript copy of the play that had been authorized by the Master of the Revels, the 'Book' that was the company's licence to perform, but that is long lost. The only authoritative text of the play that survives is that in Q1.

Whereas writing is a solitary activity, producing and publishing plays are communal activities with many social interactions and collaborations involved. A scribe wrote out the parts for the actors, and errors were possible. Changes might be introduced during the brief rehearsal period, or during subsequent performances of the play, for a variety of reasons. Any confusions in the text could be resolved, the book-keeper (what we would call stage manager or prompter) might adjust a scene to fit the company's resources, actors might invent new lines or cut unsatisfactory ones, depending on audience reaction, or the playwright himself might revise the play. In this particular play, there is evidence of the playhouse being alert to the censorship laws forbidding blasphemy: on at least 24 occasions in the play Webster's habitual use of the word 'God' appears to have been deleted in favour of 'heaven' (which could be pronounced as one syllable if the metre required). Typical examples are found at I.i.276 and III.v.100.

A similar range of interactions applied when a play was published. Webster would initially have written the play out himself, but there may have been scratchings-out, insertions, and even minor confusions, as is common in most authors' drafts, before it went to the playhouse. In the case of *The Duchess of Malfi*, it is likely that the company scribe, Raph Crane, recopied the entire play from the promptbook (which would have had more stage directions than survive in Q1) into a fair copy that was given to the printers in 1623.

Crane's tendency in his transcriptions of plays was to follow a continental European style of gathering the names of all the characters who would appear in a scene at the head of the scene, whether they were to enter immediately or only later. This system was designed for readers, not actors, and it leaves modern editors and directors with some interesting problems. Following I.i.81, for instance, Crane indicates that a new scene should start, and lists all the characters to appear from here to the end of the act. These include Castruchio's young wife (and the Cardinal's mistress) Julia, and the Duchess's waiting woman Cariola. Most modern editions (including John Russell Brown's Revels Student edition) have Julia enter with Castruchio immediately (at I.i.81.1), but she may not enter until 147.1, with the Duchess and presumably Cariola and maybe other ladies. The first decision has the virtue of providing Castruchio with an opportunity to gesture to Julia as he retells her jest instead of allowing her to do it, thereby identifying her as his wife. The second prevents Julia being thus patronized by her husband, and more importantly provides the Duchess with a more impressive retinue, probably to take her place on a state and thereby display that this is her court, not Ferdinand's. In addition, if Julia is first seen as one of the Duchess's ladies, the parallelism between them that is a marked feature later in the play can be placed early and given emphasis. At a later point in the scene, when the Duchess and the Cardinal rejoin Ferdinand at I.i.291.1, Brown's edition has no entry for Cariola. Thus the Duchess is left entirely alone to be catechized by her brothers. Certainly this staging would tend to stress her vulnerability. But when her brothers leave she almost immediately starts talking to Cariola, and there is no good reason for the stage delay of the Duchess calling for her and waiting for her to arrive before continuing her sentence (I.i.349–51). In addition, the constant attendance of waiting women would be the norm at the period; nor would it be an inhibition to her brothers speaking frankly. But again, Raph Crane has left the text theatrically unclear, so it is up to readers and performers to consider entries and exits carefully.

Then the compositors in the printing house added their contribution: adopting their own favourite spellings, inserting punctuation they thought was needed (for punctuation was at this period more the responsibility of the actor in the theatre or the compositor in the printing house than of the author, although with this play a lot of Crane's personal preferences in spelling and punctuation show through). Compositors might also misread their manuscript copy, whether because it was badly written, or because they were tired, lazy, or even drunk. Thus, given the collaborative nature of both theatre and publishing, and the continuing performance and possibly adjustment of the play, we can have very little certainty about how close the 1623 Q1 text is to what was first performed in 1613 or 1614, or to how Webster wished it to be performed.

However, we have a strong indication that Webster visited the printing house while his play was being proofread. The most striking evidence is several differences between uncorrected and corrected versions of III.iv. (Uncorrected sheets with errors discovered that needed correction were not thrown away, so printed copies of early plays typically contain uncorrected versions of some sheets in some copies, and corrected sheets in others, requiring comparison of many surviving copies of the book in order to ascertain the corrected version of each sheet.) In the uncorrected state the song that is sung as the Cardinal divests himself of his robes, and is installed as a soldier, is headed 'The Hymn', and the stage direction says '*this hymn is sung, to very solemn music, by divers* Churchmen' (III.iv.7.8–.9). In the corrected state the heading is gone, the word '*hymn*' in the SD changed to '*ditty*', and a marginal note added: 'The author disclaims this ditty to be his' (III.iv, opposite ll. 8–11). Clearly Webster was in the printing house reading proof, and left no doubt about what he thought of the words (and possibly music he may have heard at performances) that the company had provided to accompany the dumb show at Loretto. He was not going to be blamed for the ditty at all, let alone have it be thought he could regard it as a hymn. The issue reminds us that a dramatic script is never fixed; both during the playwright's life, and even afterwards, the collaborators in the play – actors, printers, audiences, and many others – ensure that the script is always ready in potential for a new manifestation, a new enactment.

The 1623 quarto of *The Duchess of Malfi* is generally a clean text, and presents few problems. It is divided into five acts. Webster, with his respect for the classics, probably had a neoclassical five-act structure in mind when writing, but it was required in any case at an indoor playhouse since act breaks allowed time for trimming candles. Nevertheless, Webster's dramaturgical thinking is likely to have been heavily influenced by the English playhouse conception of the scene: starting and ending with a cleared stage. This is the basis for his scene divisions, and is probably the most useful starting point for thinking about the structure of the play. In the modern theatre, of course, the major element defining the structure the audience experiences is where intervals are placed, and how many there are. No interval (probably how it was originally performed), one interval, two intervals, or even more: these structure the modern event, and will have a powerful impact on our reaction to the play in performance.

Another crucial area for actors, audiences, and readers is punctuation. Early modern punctuation operated by different standards to ours, and writers, scribes, and printers had different usages, and were much less punctilious than we would be. To take an example, here is a transcription of the Q1 version of III.ii.326–34 (spelling, capitalization, and typography modernized):

> A politician is the devil's quilted anvil,
> He fashions all sins on him, and the blows
> Are never heard, he may work in a lady's chamber,
> (As here for proof) what rests, but I reveal
> All to my lord? Oh, this base quality
> Of intelligencer? Why, every quality i'th'world
> Prefers but gain, or commendation:
> Now for this act, I am certain to be raised,
> "And men that paint weeds, (to the life) are praised.

Here is the same text from John Russell Brown's Revels Student edition:

> A politician is the devil's quilted anvil:
> He fashions all sins on him, and the blows
> Are never heard; he may work in a lady's chamber,
> As here for proof. What rests but I reveal
> All to my lord? O, this base quality
> Of intelligencer! Why, every quality i'th' world
> Prefers but gain or commendation:
> Now, for this act I am certain to be raised,
> *And men that paint weeds to the life are praised.*

We might divide the punctuation changes that Brown and other modern editors have made into three categories. First, those that to a modern reader appear essential to fix a Q1 error. For instance, the comma after 'heard' in the third line of the excerpt is too weak; all modern editions strengthen the punctuation, Leah Marcus even using a full stop in her Arden Early Modern Drama edition. Even worse is the absence of any punctuation in the following line after '(As here for proof)', which may initially lead a reader to think the proof applies to 'what rests'; all modern editors supply a full stop. But the first of these two examples would not have worried a Jacobean typesetter or actor, since the comma (so long as sense is clear) enables the forward pressure of Bosola's scorn to continue full flow. The absence of punctuation in the second example might well have been recognized as an error (and in a modern edition with the parentheses removed it becomes insupportable), but the presence of the closing parenthesis after 'proof' seems often to provide compositors with sufficient reason not to add any other punctuation. A final example in this category of apparent errors is the question mark following 'intelligencer' two lines further down: all modern editors change it to an exclamation mark. However, our Jacobean compositor was simply following one of the conventions of early seventeenth-century writing and printing: the question mark could represent either a query or an exclamation mark. We now distinguish between them, but it often requires editorial decision. And although all modern editors agree that this question mark indicates an exclamation rather than an interrogative, it is perhaps surprising that no editor has thought that 'What rests but I reveal / All to my lord?', despite being in the form of a question, might have an even stronger exclamatory force if it is spoken with the strong self-loathing evident in the rest of the speech.

A second category comprises the commas that interrupt the flow and structure of what in modern usage would usually be unpunctuated: 'what rests,' 'but gain,' 'this act,' and especially 'paint weeds,' once the parentheses are removed. Removal of the commas is universal by modern editors only for the final example; for all the others, the rhetorical usage of the early seventeenth century is retained by some editors but not by others.

The final category includes what appear to be double opening quote marks, or inverted commas, preceding the last line of the excerpt. But there is no closing set of inverted commas, and the ["] is not in this case a mark of punctuation, but in the technical language describing manuscripts, a 'diple', one of the marks (*notae*) that might be used to attract the reader's attention to something particular. Elsewhere in *The Duchess of Malfi* the compositors have tended to use italic type to

set apart such aphorisms or *sententiae* (sententious common knowledge) from the rest of the text, and most editors set this line too in
italics, as Brown has done. Only René Weis, in his *The Duchess of Malfi
and Other Plays* for the Oxford World's Classics series, sets the line in
roman type with no diple, as if the line were no different from what
had gone before. Marcus, in her Arden edition, interestingly retains
the diple as opening quotation marks, and provides closing quotes
to match; this solution, like the italics, catches the sense that readers
(and actors of Bosola) are expected to recognize that the thought is
self-consciously presented as a commonly known aphorism being
applied to the current situation. In performance, actors may have
stepped forward to address the audience directly, and some modern
productions have used hard-edged spotlights on Bosola to suggest
his role as an authorial mouthpiece. It is useful for actors as well as
readers to be wary about how easily we accept modernized punctuation. The collaboration with the playwright should remain active.

Another crucial element for actors is the metre. Webster's verse is
often dense and mosaic-like in its structure, demanding and repaying
close attention to its intricacy and abrupt collisions of meaning and,
often, reworking of material from other authors. There is much to
be used by actors, clues to character and stage dynamics. A passage
from III.ii, as Ferdinand is venting his violent rage on his sister for her
secret marriage, demonstrates that the playwright may offer character notes and acting advice through the verse if we are alert to the
signals. In the excerpt below a regular iambic (te-**tum**) pentameter
beat has been applied by printing in bold words or syllables that,
by their position in the line, would normally take a strong beat. The
Duchess starts by completing a line in which Ferdinand as already
supplied two beats (te-**tum**, te-**tum**, te)

Duchess.   **Why** might **not** I **mar**ry?
I **have** not **gone** a**bout**, in **this**, to **cre**ate   110
An**y** new **world** or **cus**tom.
Ferdinand.   Thou **art** un**done**;
And **thou** hast **ta'en** that **mas**sy **sheet** of **lead**
That **hid** thy **hus**band's **bones**, and **fold**ed **it**
A**bout** my **heart**.

If we take Ferdinand's reply first, we find the iambic pentameter is
utterly regular; each foot is iambic (te-**tum**), and there are exactly

five feet, ten syllables. Furthermore, the beats come on important words heavy with meaning. The effect is of an oppressive drum beat, inevitable and powerful. The actor of Ferdinand need be in no doubt how about the confidence and pressure with which he may deliver this speech.

The Duchess's speech is much more difficult to scan. The initial half line, although regular, has its force diminished somewhat by the extra syllable at the end of the line. While this unstressed ending is a very common and acceptable variation to standard iambic pentameter, its softening or weakening function has been recognized by its (unintentionally misogynistic) description as a 'feminine' ending. At the end of the second line, however, the word 'create' simply cannot be pronounced with the stress on the first syllable. Since pronunciation must be 'cre**ate**', the line ends with an anapest (te-te-**tum**), breaking the flow of the iambic pattern. The Duchess's final half line (into which the previous line runs on with no break in meaning or from punctuation) departs even further from regularity of emphasis. 'An**y**' is almost impossible to say, and although changing the iambic stress to trochaic (**A**ny) could allow for an emphatic contrapuntal **tum**-te, te-**tum**, the resultant stress (**A**ny new **world**) would lack its usual contrapuntal power because it seems to ignore the meaning: the Duchess is surely emphasizing that she has not done anything **new**. Thus the she must stress both **new** and **world**, combining a most unusual phyrric foot (te-te) with a subsequent spondee (**tum**-**tum**): 'Any **new world**'. And again she ends on an extra, unstressed syllable ('**cus**tom'), this time in the middle of the line. The total effect can be read in a number of ways, including nervousness, agitation, uncertainty, struggling to find a rhythm, fear; but the scansion does not lend itself easily to assurance, control, power – nor, as delivered by Helen Mirren in a famous 1980 production, to feminist anger.

Finally, the Q1 title page tells us that the published text is 'the perfect and exact copy, with divers things printed that the length of the play would not bear in the presentment'. In other words, the play was too long, and the actors made cuts in order to reduce the running time in performance; but Webster wanted readers of his play to have access to everything he wrote. It was common theatrical practice to cut plays run to 'the two-hours' traffic of our stage' (*Romeo and Juliet*, Prologue, l. 12) or a little more, but there is no evidence in the text what might have been cut from *The Duchess of Malfi*. The only clue we have is the informative list of 'The Actors' Names' discussed above, and while it does not tell us what was cut, it suggests that radical excision of entire scenes, or subplot, is unlikely. Of the significant speaking parts, only Castruchio and the Old Lady are left out. Julia, the Doctor, the Madmen, and the Pilgrims are all included. Busino reports the presence of both the Julia subplot and the dumb show at Loretto. It therefore seems that whatever cuts were made in early performances were likely to be the pruning of speeches or shortening of scenes, and not drastic structural change.

Discussion of the text of the play serves to remind us that it is fluid, in a sense always in process. For actors, it is the starting point towards performance, full of clues and possibilities and potential each time the play is presented. Spectators, whether familiar or unfamiliar with the play, still experience it moment by moment, as it unfolds in time as performance.

Note

The Duchess of Malfi by John Webster is quoted and referred to in this book from the Revels Student edition edited by John Russell Brown (Manchester and New York: Manchester University Press, 1997), based on his Revels Plays edition (London: Methuen, 1964; 2nd edition Manchester and New York; Manchester University Press, 2009). In common with other Handbooks in this series, all references to Shakespeare plays are to the Oxford *Complete Works*, edited by Stanley Wells and Gary Taylor (1986), and the *Norton Shakespeare* that is based upon it with Stephen Greenblatt as its general editor (1997).

2 Commentary: The Play in Performance

Introduction

The Duchess of Malfi is divided into five acts, but act divisions were a recent innovation at the time (see pp. 11–12). Playwrights tended to write in scenes, probably pretty much as the scene divisions appear in modern editions of the play. These are 'English scenes' – scenes that continue until all characters exit, leaving the stage clear for a new scene to begin. Generally speaking an English scene, long or short, contains a complete episode. Yet for purposes of analysis (and probably for Webster when writing), it is useful to consider what we now call 'French scenes' – scenes that continue only until any character leaves the stage, or any new character enters. Act V, scene i, for instance, is a single English scene but contains five French scenes. The difference in stage activity, mood, rhythm, and content between the first and last French scenes, with just the two close friends Antonio and Delio talking alone; the second and fourth scenes, in which Antonio observes Delio testing the Marquis of Pescara's integrity; and the central third scene, in which Pescara gives Antonio's confiscated lands to a courtesan as a moral lesson to Delio; these structural divisions give a clear sense of the importance of French scenes as units of playmaking and analysis. They are also usually the basic units of rehearsal of a play.

The commentary that follows takes French scenes as the initial unit for analysis, but often needs to subdivide the French scene into what may be called 'units of action'. These units of action are usually initiated by a significant change in subject or stage dynamic. Taking V.i as an example again, after a discussion between Antonio and Delio about the confiscation of Antonio's lands, a new French scene starts with the entry of Pescara at l. 14.1. Antonio agrees to overhear Delio confronting Pescara. When Delio advances alone at l. 18 to find out what Pescara is doing with Antonio's lands, it is a new unit of action because the dynamic on stage has changed from two friends observing the entrance of a possible enemy to one of them eavesdropping while the other engages the new arrival. The entry of Julia starts a new French scene and by definition a new unit, both of which end when she leaves. The fourth French scene ends with the exit of Pescara, though one could argue that Delio's acceptance at l. 54 of Pescara's homily about honourable behaviour ends one unit of action, and that the few lines on a new topic before Pescara exits constitute a new unit of action. Then follows the final French scene (and unit of action) until Antonio and Delio exit together, ending the unit of action, the fifth French scene, and the English scene V.i.

Awareness of French scenes and units of action will assist readers of this commentary to visualize the shift in theatrical dynamics at the point of change from one unit to another; this is the underlying structure of the play in performance.

Act I

Note: Decimal points following a line number indicate a stage direction following that line. Thus 'l. 14.1' signals the first line of a stage direction following line 14.

Act I, scene i

1–4 Two men enter. On a bare Jacobean stage, only their words, clothes, props, perhaps music and black stage hangings for tragedy, and possibly attendants or others on stage, can inform us of what kind of play we are to see. On a modern stage, set or lighting may provide additional emotional colouring and social context. Delio is welcoming his 'dear Antonio' home (the name suggests Italy, as does the play's title). Does Delio see him for the first time now, or do they enter together deep in conversation? Delio seems eager for news, and observes that Antonio is dressed as 'A very formal Frenchman' (l. 3). As gentlemen, both will be wearing rich clothing, hats, and rapiers. But if Antonio continues an obvious outsider in his foreign fashion at court, this will strongly influence our view of him and the Duchess later. Also related to dress code is whether Antonio is wearing a steward's chain of office, as befits 'the great master' (l. 89) of the Duchess's household. In some productions there is visual evidence he has just come from the tiltyard, whether by still carrying his lance or gauntlets from riding for the 'ring' (l. 87), wearing boots and spurs (unlike other courtiers in this scene perhaps), or mopping his brow from his exertions.

4–22 Antonio's long speech in praise of the French king and court introduces the first serious thematic material of the play. Whether or not the two men are alone on stage, it will be significant if they choose to lower their voices, or move away from any potential listeners. Is this a court at which it is dangerous to be heard praising a ruler who encourages his courtiers to speak honestly in warning him of 'flatt'ring sycophants' (l. 8) and corruption? Note that the parenthetical comment in lines 9–10 ('which…heaven') is awkward in syntax; 'which' seems to refer grammatically to 'infamous persons', but in fact refers to the entire preceding sentence – the cleansing of the court. The line is therefore often cut, though the concept of divine guidance is significant. In 1960 the Stratford production had a large fountain on stage that realistically allowed Antonio to mop his brow from the exertion of the tilt, and symbolically encouraged the audience to consider the elaborate metaphor about the dangers of corruption flowing through the whole land from 'a common fountain' (l. 12).

22–28 Bosola's entry interrupts Antonio and Delio and marks the start of a new 'French scene'. They observe and comment on him as a hypocrite who rails against corruption at court only because he himself does not benefit. Bosola's clothing, though that of a gentleman, is likely to signal what is later confirmed: poverty from lack of reward for his services. He may wear black, the 'old garb of melancholy' (l. 278); he is often costumed in leather, suggesting soldiering, and in the 1971 production at the Canadian Stratford Festival his attire was described as symbolically eaten away as if with corrosive acid.

This is the first of a series of such observations as significant characters enter, and usually requires either that Antonio and Delio have now taken up a position on stage from which they can comment unheard (such as a balcony, or a corner of the stage); or a degree of stylization, such as having the new characters freeze as they are described.

29–40 We observe Antonio and Delio observing this tense encounter in which Bosola approaches a prince of the church, a cardinal identifiable by his scarlet robes and wide-brimmed hat. Whether or not Bosola kneels to kiss the Cardinal's ring (sometimes demanded by the Cardinal), Bosola switches from verse to direct, rude prose. And despite the Cardinal's brief, cold dismissals, Bosola perseveres in demanding reward for jobs he has done 'in your service' (l. 34). Evidently these jobs were criminal, for Bosola has been sentenced to hard labour as a galley oarsman (for two years he says, though Delio says later seven, for 'a notorious murder' [l. 70]). But as a character, Bosola has an attractive self-awareness, acknowledging (perhaps raising a laugh) that he is an 'arrant knave' (l. 42).

41–68 The Cardinal probably leaves the stage, but may simply withdraw. Bosola seems to turn to Antonio and Delio as he identifies the Cardinal as worse than he himself: able to corrupt the devil. Bosola needs little encouragement to rail at the Cardinal and his brother as examples of precisely the opposite of the French king: powerful men who encourage parasites rather than honest advisors. And in striking and grotesque metaphysical imagery, he paints a picture of a dog-eat-dog world in which every man kicks the man below him.

69–81 A director may choose, as with the Cardinal, whether Bosola exits or joins a gradually swelling group of attendants and courtiers awaiting Duke Ferdinand and the Duchess. Either way, Antonio and Delio are effectively alone. Delio suggests that Bosola is more corrupt and dangerous than Bosola himself admitted, but Antonio modifies his previous condemnation (ll. 23–9) by blaming Bosola's malcontent behaviour on his melancholy (in Renaissance psychology, one of the four 'humours', a disposition to be obsessive and pessimistic, brought on by an excess of black bile in the body). The malcontent was by now a standard figure in the drama, a figure at court who defined himself as an outsider by ignoring court decorum, and offering scathing and unwanted advice to anyone who came in his path. And Webster himself had a hand in expanding John Marston's *The Malcontent* (1603). Antonio thus suggests that virtue is not inherent in Bosola or anyone else, but must be nurtured and given activity. The political and social context is culpable otherwise.

82 to the end   *This long section, identified as a separate scene in Q1, has four main movements: the formal presence chamber action in which the Duchess holds court for her two brothers, and they are anatomized by Antonio; Duke Ferdinand's suborning of Bosola to spy upon the Duchess; Ferdinand and the Cardinal's warning to the widowed Duchess not to marry again; and her immediate defiance of their warning by wooing Antonio into a secret marriage.*

82–6   This can be played as beginning a new 'English scene' – the stage cleared before it starts, as (probably mistakenly) printed in Q1. It is more often treated as a continuation of I.i, since Antonio and Delio seem to continue their observation of the courtiers entering 'The presence' (i.e., the presence chamber, a room in which a ruler would formally be 'in presence' on a raised 'state' or throne, and conduct business). Costuming and behaviour will say much about how tightly constrained the court is by ritual, fear, or custom. In addition, Castruchio's age will be evident from his white beard, and his profession from the lawyer's coif on his head (see II.i.1–23). Because Q1 lists at this point all the characters who appear in this long scene, it is uncertain how many enter here. Clearly the Cardinal and the Duchess do not enter until l. 147.1. Most editions of the play have Castruchio's young wife Julia enter now, but she is just as likely to enter later attending on the Duchess (see pp. 9–10 and 127).

86–90   The abruptness with which Ferdinand, 'the great Calabrian duke' (no doubt very richly attired; and sometimes, in modern productions, with fur about the costume that only later will be understood to prefigure his particular madness), instructs an unnamed subordinate to give Antonio the prize for winning the tournament often seems aristocratic hauteur.

90–147   As Ferdinand exchanges wit and banter with his courtiers, several aspects of his character become apparent. The circle around him will be deferential, but the old Castruchio (whose very name suggests sexual inadequacy) is the first to respond to the duke's suggestion that they should go to war ('fall to action', l. 91) by urging a serious objection to a ruler being a soldier. Ferdinand diverts the conversation into a slightly bawdy retelling of a joke made by Castruchio's wife. (If she is present, and presumably much younger than Castruchio, Ferdinand may be openly flirting with her.) When Roderigo and Silvio start to add their own wit, however, Ferdinand explicitly demands that they defer to him, only 'take fire when I give fire' (l. 123–4). This may be a serious demand that they be sycophantic (the opposite of what Antonio praised as the virtue of the French court), but more often the lightning shift from geniality to mocking antagonism leaves the courtiers shocked and uneasy. It also allows the actor to lay the groundwork for Ferdinand's later overt madness.

148–51 When the Duchess enters with the Cardinal (perhaps accompanied by Julia and Cariola, and maybe other courtiers or attendants), the courtiers probably all kneel (their hats already off, since the presence chamber requires it), but her two brothers may assert their greater power by remaining standing. She may be in black, befitting a widow, or in brighter colours suiting the recent tournament and the 'chargeable revels' (l. 333). The actors will have options about how much to play the formality of the occasion, how much to play the sibling relationship. Does the audience see the Duchess as tense or relaxed, formal or playful? Ferdinand immediately presents Silvio to her, just as later he will suggest promotion for Bosola. Silvio's leave-taking is presumably in dumb-show, allowing Antonio and Delio to comment on the Duchess and her two brothers.

152–67 The Cardinal is the first of the siblings to be anatomized. At this point it may be most obvious that all three are much of an age. Family resemblance may be powerfully assisted by wigs; Ferdinand and the Duchess as twins may both have the same hair colour. Staging may shift audience attention onto each of the three in turn by using realist techniques, such as the major figure moving to talk to someone else, thereby taking a dominant position on stage; or may use techniques of stylization such as spotlighting, dumb-show tableaux, or even frozen action so that Delio and Antonio can move among them as if they were statues at a museum. Each is isolated and analysed, like a rare species under a microscope, and the audience is likely to compare what is said now with what they have already seen and heard.

Delio knows the Cardinal's reputation as a playboy – gambling, party-going, womanizing, duelling – which suggests a cheerfully secular and pleasure-loving prince of the church. This characteristic may be evident if he is flirting with Castruchio's wife Julia, who, we learn later, is his mistress. Antonio responds that he is not what he seems; that he is melancholic (though later he appears more coldly phlegmatic) and treacherous. His corrupt methods include hiring spies, entrapment of enemies, and attempting to bribe his way to the papacy. Despite appearing a churchman, 'the devil speaks' in him (l. 186).

168–86   As attention shifts to Duke Ferdinand the audience may remember his unpredictable behaviour with his courtiers, and his control of 'mirth' (l. 170). Antonio now describes the Cardinal's brother as his twin 'in quality' (l. 172): similarly devious, hypocritical, and Machiavellian. His external mirth is a deliberate pose to mislead his enemies, whom he will entrap using information from his spies. In particular, he will manipulate the law to his own ends, as the powerful can do. Antonio's brief return to speaking of the Cardinal reinforces the sense of the two brothers being linked (just as they may be side by side on stage at this point), as does the short line with which comment on them ends. This may indicate a pause before Antonio, finished with the two men, now turns to a more positive appraisal of their sister.

187–209   Delio asked for descriptions of the two brothers, but Antonio moves on to speak of the Duchess unprompted. He seems to acknowledge the likely stylized tableau of the three siblings on stage when he speaks of them as 'three fair medals / Cast in one figure' (ll. 188–89). The image is of molten metal cast in a single mould three times to produce the same the same facial characteristics ('figure') and general appearance in all three, but with the Duchess of a different 'temper' (punning on tempering metal). Antonio praises her speech in terms more suitable to a courtly lover than an objective observer. He reinforces this with extravagant praise for her looks, which would lead anyone to 'dote' (l. 197), and finally denies what has not been asserted – that her sexual virtue is anything other than admirable. Delio responds as the audience may in thinking Antonio to be somewhat excessive in his praise, but Antonio repeats that she is unique in the world, perfection itself.

209–12   That Cariola, a waiting-woman, should arrive at this very moment, just as Antonio finishes his encomium to the Duchess, to summon him to attend the Duchess, seems to be structurally deliberate, drawing audience attention to the artifice of the coincidence.

213–23   Suddenly the main court group comes back to bustling life, first with an important plot element: Ferdinand securing Bosola a high place in the household of the Duchess. Then Ferdinand's declared intention of taking his leave of Malfi introduces brief reference to Silvio departing for a military camp at Milan, and indeed the entire court follows the Duchess to see off the visitors. Trumpet flourishes or other production business may emphasize such a major transition. The sudden emptying of the stage closes a long section, and leaves just the Cardinal and Ferdinand. In modern productions a lighting change may further suggest what is virtually a new scene.

224–31   This brief exchange may be made to seem secretive, by lowered voices, suspicious glances, or isolating lighting. The Cardinal is every bit as Machiavellian as Antonio warned, and the audience will need to revise its opinion of his rejection of Bosola earlier in the scene: it was much more subtle, and more duplicitous, than it appeared. The Cardinal also chides Ferdinand for being naïve, and failing to recognize that Antonio is too honest to be useful to them. The entry of Bosola at this moment seems another deliberate irony – here is a man who is not too honest.

231–46   Ferdinand follows his brother's plan by insisting that the Cardinal is hostile to him, and that all powerful men do well to be suspicious. Bosola responds with malcontent rudeness and directness, and has the last word about true and false suspicion. His coarseness and refusal to defer in the face of aristocratic arrogance can make him a very attractive figure to the audience, and casting a powerful, sympathetic, and humorous actor is crucial.

246–66   'There's gold' says Ferdinand (l. 246). The actor playing Bosola has choices about how the character will respond, in particular whether he physically accepts what is probably a purse of gold, how much he plays for comedy. The reply 'Whose throat must I cut?' will usually raise a laugh, but whether Bosola's two lines preceding that repartee are aside to the audience or direct to Antonio will influence audience reaction. Ferdinand at ll. 250–51 is also ironically humorous as the two men take the measure of each other. The nature of Ferdinand's offer is straightforward – Bosola is to spy on the Duchess, especially on any intention to remarry – but Bosola's refusal is a surprise. The rejection can be physical, if he throws the purse to the stage. The relationship between the two men is edgy, usually reinforced by Ferdinand's refusal, without really being asked, to reveal the motives for his opposition to his sister remarrying. The actor will need to decide whether indeed he does consciously know.

267–88   Ferdinand's refusal to accept the gold back makes Bosola realize that he has been outmanoeuvred. The Provisorship of the Horse (a position of some responsibility, with opportunity for enrichment) is just the kind of place at court for which he was desperate. Now he has it, but at a price that requires him to swallow his moral scruples about becoming a paid spy. Interestingly for the actor and the audience, he does not hide his disgust, but makes a coarse joke about being corrupted by horse dung. To his accusation that Ferdinand is acting like the devil (as does the Cardinal), Ferdinand praises Bosola's malcontent pose of melancholy, and says it will be a useful cover for spying. Ferdinand reiterates his instructions that Bosola should eavesdrop and glean intelligence at the Duchess's court, but again he fails to say why.

289–91   Although there is no stage direction for Ferdinand to exit, he may see the Duchess approaching and move away. Bosola probably addresses his rhyming-couplet *sententia* (see pp. 13–14) as a general comment to the audience rather than to Ferdinand, thereby drawing the audience to him, and he has the option of playing it as stand-up comedy. An audience will always respond to villainy if the villain is not only open but also funny. In his ironic final line before he exits Bosola acknowledges that he, too, is now a devil, but that he may preach the truth on occasion.

292–328   Modern productions and screen versions usually change lighting or even setting for what is virtually a new English scene as the Cardinal, Duchess, and probably Cariola enter to join Ferdinand. The verbal structure is of a catechism: formalized religious teaching of moral law. Usually staging will reflect this formality by placing Ferdinand and the Cardinal symmetrically either side of the Duchess as they alternate (again quasi-religious in verse-and-response structure) in offering precepts of why she should not remarry. It is notable that although they both express an apparent abhorrence of second marriages, the Cardinal stresses 'honour' (l. 296), implicitly emphasizing their Aragonian royal blood, whereas Ferdinand starts with her sexual experience ('You know...what man is', 'luxurious', ll. 294, 297), then moves from whoredom to the corruption of the court, the hypocrisy of secrecy, and eventually returns to 'lustful pleasures' (l. 326). Given their criticism, the suggestion from the Cardinal that she may please herself by taking a lover in secret seems a clear example of the hypocrisy Ferdinand warned against.

A vital element is the way in which the Duchess reacts. She starts with a playful counter-argument about diamonds that pass through many hands, and then says 'I'll never marry' (l. 302). This appears an absolute denial; but she may be interrupted half way through this short verse line (see p. 126). Either way, the Duchess will have to decide how seriously to take her brothers' warnings, and how much of her own emotions to let them see.

329–40   The Duchess accuses Ferdinand of conspiring with the Cardinal on the lecture they have just delivered. It may be significant that she has waited until the Cardinal has left. The tone may be light-hearted and teasing, anxious, or even fearful. She soon has reason to fear, for her brother's implied threat to use his dagger on her is clear, as he demands she stop wasting money on court festivities. Some productions have the Duchess from her first entrance holding a 'visor', not only to emphasize her active social life, but also to add weight to Ferdinand's assertion that secrets (cf. 'whispering-rooms') are incompatible with 'goodness' (ll. 334–35). The sexuality of Ferdinand's language is striking and unsettling. He implies her attraction to a penis even as he claims to be talking about lampreys and tongues, and given this language it will be difficult for an audience not to perceive the poniard too as phallic. His farewell to his sister as 'lusty widow' is in some productions accompanied by an overtly sexual kiss, but there is a danger of rendering reductively incestuous the motivation and actions of which Ferdinand seems scarcely aware at a conscious level.

341–9   Brown's edition of the play delays Cariola's entrance until l. 349.1, which means that the Duchess is alone on stage as she declares that she will ignore her brothers' demands. Even if her waiting woman has been in attendance since her entry with the Cardinal, the Duchess may still be addressing the audience. Her language of danger and battle makes clear she is aware of the danger; the audience may admire her determination, but they can hardly fail to recognize what is at best recklessness and at worst dangerous foolishness.

349–61   In this brief transition both Cariola's support and loyalty for her mistress and the Duchess's very human apprehension about the course she is embarking on alone are likely to evoke audience sympathy. Cariola confirms that Antonio is in attendance, and the Duchess instructs her to hide behind the arras to eavesdrop (cf. Polonius hiding behind the arras in *Hamlet* III.iv). Some productions have Cariola open a door for Antonio prior to hiding herself, which may encourage a lighter mood than the alternative; if the Duchess is left alone on stage (possibly for ll. 358–61 as well), and lets Antonio in herself, unattended, her trepidation can be stressed and Antonio's initial, perhaps surprised, silence may be explained.

361–409   In this section of the long French scene in which the Duchess woos Antonio she will still be in her elaborate court dress from earlier in the act, whereas Antonio's subordinate status will be visually evident not just from his steward's chain of office, but also from the writing materials he must be carrying when he enters. The Duchess gradually leads him from her actual accounts to talking of the future and whether she should remarry. Her language is playfully full of puns ('husband', 'for your sake', 'couple', 'will'; ll. 366, 369, 389, 390). It is not clear if he understands her drift, and there is brief comedy as she punningly teases him about standing up to fetch her accounts ('upright'; l. 372). On the other hand, he praises her beauty early on, and himself puns on wedding sheets and 'will'. His weak assertion of being indifferent to marriage and fatherhood, however, drives the Duchess to unequivocal (but still punning) language and action: giving him a ring to improve his eyesight, and telling him it is a wedding ring to be given only to her second husband.

Important acting decisions face both actors. Antonio may stress his class difference and deference (or reluctance) by his posture and attitude, and by standing, and then sitting, at a distance. This approach would align with William Rowley's commendatory verse in which he refers to the Duchess's 'low-rated (i.e., socially inferior) love'. Such an interpretation is likely to require the Duchess to take the initiative physically as well as verbally. Some productions, however, have stressed Antonio's overt attraction or even lust for the Duchess. Tension because both are nervous will emphasize the danger they face (and tend to make Antonio look weak, which may be appropriate), whereas a sense that they often enjoy banter together will allow the comedy to surface, and a more romantic portrayal of their mutual attraction. For example, in nineteenth-century productions the Duchess was usually arch, and laughing with playful coquetry.

410–15   This brief verbal and physical sequence around the wedding ring marks the moment at which double entendre gives way to an overt offer of marriage by the Duchess. The puns on blindness and eyesight, on conjuring circles and the ring, now have a serious edge as Antonio declares the attraction and danger of ambition. As she puts the matter beyond doubt by placing her wedding ring on his finger, he kneels (in confusion? deference? fear? joy?); and these two physical acts signal a new reality.

416–40   Antonio understands 'whereto your favours tend' (l. 426), but he does not respond with emotion, but rather with an insistence on the dangers inherent in her offer: only the 'great man' (l. 420) can afford secret pleasures. A liaison that is not open and publicly approved is, he says, 'lunatic' (l. 424). He stresses his 'unworthiness' (l. 430), his lower social status. His costume, compared to hers, may be an important clue as to whether the characters (or the production) engage with class difference as seriously as the Duchess's brothers do. In some productions Antonio is dressed in drab or even puritan clothing, in striking contrast to aristocratic finery worn by the Duchess. In others, lack of significant contrast throws more attention on to subtext, on to whether or not Antonio is really resistant and fearful, and onto the psychological makeup of the Duchess. She tells him he is a 'complete man', refusing to engage with the class issue, but rather praising him as the wearer of the 'sovereign' (l. 405) wedding ring when she instructs him to make a (royal) 'progress' (l. 437) through himself. Antonio's reply, that he is determined to remain 'honest' (l. 438; i.e., virtuous) seems to be a rejection of an offer that virtue requires him to refuse. At this point the sequence might end; an offer has been made and refused. How can the Duchess go further? And for the actor of Antonio, with what mixture of admiration, self-respect, love, lust, or fear does he stand in silence now as the Duchess decides what to do next?

440–59 The Duchess bemoans (sincerely, or possibly playfully) her high rank as forcing her to take the initiative, and equates her indirect language with leaving 'the path / Of simple virtue' (ll. 446–7). She seems to echo Antonio's fear of departing from 'fair, lightsome lodgings' (l. 422). Her apparent admission of failure – 'go brag / You have left me heartless' (l. 449) – may however be accompanied by physical contact, since she at this point realizes that he is trembling. Although her attribution of his trembling to fear rather than passion may surprise us, continuing physical contact seems implied by her reference to her own body ('*This* is flesh and blood', l. 453), and her most direct and passionate words follow as she 'claims [him] for her husband' (l. 458). By announcing she does so as 'a young widow', she may remind us of the Cardinal and Ferdinand's implied criticism of her sexual experience and appetite; or modern audiences may respond more to her loving (or lustful) defiance of the conventional constrictions of class and gender.

459–75 Antonio's promise to protect the Duchess's good name is clearly acceptance of marriage, visually reinforced almost immediately by her kissing him and clasping him in her arms ('this circumference', l. 469). This is nevertheless punningly based on his lower rank as her steward, since her kiss is his *Quietus* – the approval of accounts and therefore his discharge from obligation. His fear of her brothers' opinion emphasizes the danger of contravening aristocratic social expectations, but usually the dominant mood of this scene is of warm and even playful tenderness as she teases and reassures him; or in some recent productions, a physical and erotic release of previous constraint. The close involvement of each with the other is broken by her request that he kneel again, and by the ending of this long French scene by the unexpected entry from behind the arras of Cariola.

476–503 Antonio's exclamation of surprise (or alarm) may be given more force if he has already knelt, and now springs up again. The Duchess clearly wants Cariola present as a witness to add weight to their marriage *per verba de praesenti* (Latin, 'by words, as from the present'; see Chapter 3, pp. 92–3). Technically she is right that their declaration will be 'absolute marriage' legally, but the church could increasingly 'force more', since both church and society (and sometimes on stage, Cariola) disapproved of such irregular marriages (ll. 479, 488). Usually the Duchess and Antonio kneel together to join right hands in the traditional 'handfast', an emblematic 'Gordian' knot, never to be untied unless severed by 'violence' (l. 480). (The 'loving palms' at l. 485–6 are not their hands, but palm trees, another 'emblem of a peaceful marriage'.) They probably stand up before the Duchess tells Cariola (who has probably assisted her to rise) to move away, and herself seems to use the space to adopt a formal emblematic pose as blind Fortune, one hand covering her eyes, the other outstretched for Antonio. Although first playfully suggesting that a naked sword will be laid between them to prevent sex, she is clearly inviting him to lead her to bed to consummate the marriage. Her wish to 'shroud her blushes' suggests that she may bury her head in his embrace as they exit, but many possibilities are open to the actors.

504–6 This tiny French scene is usually the first time a character has been alone on stage, which will give emphasis to Cariola's mixture of admiration and fear for the Duchess. She usually watches them leave before turning to the audience, and therefore her words, full of foreboding, are like the explanation under the picture in a traditional emblem book. She sees the Duchess as divided between the forces of 'greatness' (l. 504; usually regarded as a male attribute) and womanhood. If those two forces are mutually exclusive, the audience may well share Cariola's pity at the danger the Duchess's rash action is likely to bring.

Act II

Act II, scene i

1 to the end   *Following the structural pause of the act break and music in early productions at the Blackfriars, this first scene of the new act has two main movements, very different in tone from each other. First, Bosola satirizes in turn Castruchio, the Old Lady, and Antonio, passing time while they await the arrival of the Duchess. The second section involves Bosola testing if the Duchess is pregnant, her hasty departure, and Delio's desperate advice to Antonio.*

1–23   Bosola and Castruchio probably enter together, Bosola with the basket of apricots he will need. He is often in new and more fashionable clothing, signalling his rise in fortune, and both Castruchio's professional status and his greater age should also be evident from costume and makeup. Glances towards the entry through which the Duchess eventually appears can indicate that they are waiting; and since this French scene has no plot function, Bosola's satire on lawyers can operate as stand-alone comedy. The reference in the first line to 'an eminent courtier' is an unusual usage by Webster referring to one who attends a law court (in addition to the obvious sense in which Castruchio attends in the Duchess's court). Early productions would have had law students in the audience to whom the legal jokes would especially appeal. Modern productions can seldom find an equivalent to Castruchio's lawyer's coif ('nightcap', ll. 5, 23), and therefore often cut the sequence, but at some cost to the development of Bosola's character as a malcontent 'court-gall' (I.i.23), and to the thematic importance of 'eminent' persons, and of perversions of justice later. If it is not cut, the emphasis is often on the other sense of 'nightcap', as worn in bed, and as hiding his long ears and by implication the cuckold's horns that can be expected by an old man with a young wife. Castruchio seems to miss this scornful meaning, and to foolishly enjoy Bosola's cruel teasing.

25–47   This second French scene initially parallels the first as the Old Lady replaces old Castruchio as a target for Bosola's satire. Attacks on cosmetics ('painting', l. 24) are common in drama of the period (cf. *Hamlet* III.i.53–5), but this is especially virulent and disgusting. Nevertheless, Bosola's persona as a railing malcontent is usually attractive to an audience, and some of the harsh images (such as the 'abortive hedgehog' of l. 32) are genuinely comic in performance. If the Old Lady's appearance matches Bosola's grotesque description, some of the comic and misogynistic edge of his attack will be dissipated, but comparison with the young Duchess in the scene just finished requires that this court lady be cast in a different mould. Similarly, as Bosola turns his attention to Castruchio as well, his mordant attack on two old people for the lechery and sexually transmitted diseases of their youth is in sharp contrast to the joyful love at the end of Act I. The arc of Bosola's thought – from makeup to the ingredients, to the plague, and to venereal disease – leads him to his 'meditation' (l. 47).

47–65   Bosola now shifts from standard satire on lawyers, cosmetics and women to a more introspective (and religiously derived) meditation on human form and life as fleeting and decaying into corruption. His shift from prose to verse may also imply a shift to direct address to the audience for what is in effect a non-naturalistic set piece; if so, he is no longer attacking or performing for Castruchio and the Old Lady, but telling the audience what he really thinks, and inviting them to share both his self-loathing and his clear unflinching view of the world. He may even gesture that the old couple constitute a point of reference. When he clearly addresses them again, returning to sardonic prose, he tells Castruchio that Julia has gone to Rome, and that therefore he is free to 'couple' with the Old Lady, before they both go to the hot mineral springs at Lucca to cure the inevitable further venereal disease. Contempt or laughter in Bosola's last two lines is usually enough to make them exit immediately.

66–74   Returning to direct address in a brief French scene in which he is alone, Bosola lists for the audience the classic symptoms of pregnancy: morning sickness, digestive upsets, circles under the eyes, a swelling belly, and unfashionable clothing that may disguise the pregnancy. Since he is not quite sure, Bosola confides to the audience that he has brought some early apricots (which he presumably displays), with which he hopes to 'discover' (l. 72; i.e., uncover) the truth.

74–111   The entry of Antonio and Delio initiates another French scene. That Delio has only just learned of Antonio's secret marriage, and is now sworn to secrecy, suggests that he may just have arrived at

Malfi for the first time since Act I, a period, as we shall learn, at least approaching nine months; recent arrival may be signalled by boots, spurs, and a riding cape. Antonio may have richer clothing than before (cf. III.i.28–9), probably now Italian rather than French (cf. I.i.2–3), although no doubt still wearing his steward's chain of office. Antonio's comment on Bosola's 'contemplation' (l. 79) indicates that Bosola has been giving the impression of not listening; and clearly he does not hear Delio's words about the marriage.

Antonio's rude opening is openly critical, but Bosola responds with elaborate apparent courtesy and self-deprecation that is actually sharp mockery of Antonio and his position as the chief officer of the court and favourite of the Duchess. He introduces astrological and genealogical terminology in a discussion of the difference between the lowly and the great – as a malcontent, he can be expected to reject social standing as indicating merit – in ways that echo thematic concerns raised in Act I by Bosola, by Ferdinand and the Cardinal, and by Antonio and the Duchess. By the time the Duchess enters, the tension between the two men will usually be quite high.

112–32   Since the entry of the Duchess is apparently a formal presence chamber, like I.i.147–222, it is likely that Grisolan and Roderigo are among the attendants, and possibly Castruchio and the Old Lady; she may even be the 'tedious lady' (l. 118). When the Duchess enters she immediately asks Antonio for his arm, which as they both know offers a private pleasure, perhaps enhanced by being apparently a courtly service. He may assist her up the few steps to her 'state'. The Duchess may play the line about being fat and short-winded as an aside to Antonio, or as a public smokescreen to deflect interest in her swelling belly. When she speaks to Bosola about acquiring a litter, perhaps calling him to her other side, his all-too-acute response forces her to deflect attention by calling to one of her ladies to fix her ruff, thereby displacing Bosola. Secret meanings continue between the Duchess and Antonio (as at her entrance) even as they apparently discuss matters of courtly interest: in this case – amongst her male courtiers all standing bare-headed – whether or not the men should doff their hats 'In the presence' (l. 124). The Duchess secretly encourages Antonio to 'stand bare' (as he does with her sexually), but he is discrete and correct in his answers, perhaps uneasy at her recklessness. Bosola feels it the moment to intervene.

133–55 Bosola may cross to the Duchess to give her the 'apricocks' (l. 134), or she may display sudden energy in rising or even crossing to him; he is observing her closely, and confides in the audience his pleasure at seeing her excitement, an apparent symptom of pregnancy. The fact that they are early fruit is stressed (since green fruit would severely test a pregnant woman's digestion, and had indeed been known to induce early labour). Indeed, as the Duchess eats them 'greedily' (l. 151; in some productions this is relatively decorous, in others the feeding of a gross appetite), Bosola offers a typically coarse explanation about the gardener ripening the apricots in horse dung. Whether or not it is true (and it could be), this comment after she has started to eat them, unpared, will always bring a laugh from the audience (seldom from the courtiers), who appreciate Bosola's irreverence. The Duchess's offer of an apricot to Antonio may have various motivations, and the actor of Antonio has to decide whether there is value in getting an easy laugh by showing that he is thinking of the horse dung when he declines. She evidently does not, since she again hints at a private meaning, this time around the word 'dainties' (l. 147), referring publicly to a delicacy to eat, but secretly to sexual pleasure.

Bosola is able to respond to the Duchess with innuendo about grafting trees to produce unexpected fruit, but then shares with the increasingly complicit audience his triumph at having confirmed that she is pregnant.

156–63 As the Duchess is seized with abdominal cramps the scene disintegrates into confusion, which may be emphasized by servants rushing on with torches as the cry 'Lights' (ll. 162, 163) demands, the Duchess rushing off escorted by her ladies in waiting, and by the immediate and disorderly exit of everyone else on stage except Antonio and Delio. In modern productions lighting changes or discordant sound effects may heighten the sense of panic. Bosola alone knows what is going on, and his calm speech is presumably matched by his sharing his awareness with the audience.

164 to the end Antonio's response to the emergency is panicky and negative, starting with 'we are lost' and ending with the same (ll. 164, 177). This is consistent with the Duchess's comment about his 'fear' (I.i.452), although in most productions it will come as a surprise, because of audience sympathy for the Duchess's wooing and marriage to Antonio. So far he has been seen in an almost entirely positive light, despite being surrounded by power and corruption. Delio, however, is cool in the crisis, and quickly advises Antonio to smuggle the midwife into the palace, and to accuse Bosola of poisoning the Duchess.

Act II, scene ii

1 to the end *The structure and rhythm of this scene are, unlike the play up until this point, broken, uneven, constantly interrupted, with many short French scenes as characters enter and leave under stress.*

1–28 Bosola's brief first speech (back in prose) to the audience suggests that hardly any time has passed since the previous scene, since he enters as soon as Delio and Antonio have gone. And in modern performance the Old Lady is nearly always the midwife mentioned by Delio a few moments earlier, often carrying a midwife's bag, or even forceps, to identify her. (This is unlikely to have been Webster's intention, since she is a 'Lady', not a midwife, who presumably would be identifiable by Bosola – hence the need for her to be smuggled in.) Whether or not she is the midwife, her dramaturgical role is no doubt to be hurrying to attend the Duchess, and therefore she is likely to be crossing the stage towards the exit the Duchess used at the end of II.i. Her first two lines suggest that Bosola is blocking her way or actually holding her. He can do this in hope of provoking her into revealing more information about the Duchess's pregnancy, and then dismiss her (after subjecting her again to a dose of his misogynistic satire about women and their sexual motivations – 'pure love' or 'precious reward'; ll. 17–18) when he realizes she has nothing to tell him.

29–33 Antonio enters with a great sense of urgency (sometimes reinforced by a bell sounding the alarm), either with – or for a stronger sense of emergency, meeting – Roderigo and Grisolan. His orders send Grisolan off to summon the other officers of the court, and in many productions Roderigo to find Forobosco (probably the name of one of the Officers about to enter). Antonio and Delio often exit at this point as well, so that rumours build in their absence. (Because of

Q1 massed entries for characters in a scene, it is impossible to be sure who Webster wanted onstage at which point; see pp. 9–10).

34–49   This brief section, often a separate French scene if Antonio and Delio and others have left (see note above), may appear merely an excuse for more sexual jesting, but the ludicrous specifics of the reported Swiss terrorist mercenary with his codpiece specially designed to hide his pistol and bullets serves effectively to demonstrate the atmosphere of uncertainty, rumour, and fear that is rife in the Duchess's court. Bosola's laughter may be at the comedy of the description, or at the officers who believe such rumours, but his concern that his apricots might be poisoned echoes the charge that Delio urged Antonio to level at him.

50–67   Whether or not Antonio, Delio, Grisolan and Roderigo re-enter now, or have been present during the Switzer report (to which Antonio makes no reference), this is in effect a new French scene as Antonio takes charge. Establishing that all the Officers are present, he gives an elaborate report (that the audience will assume is simply an invented story) of lost plate and jewellery. He also ensures the palace is locked, and orders everyone to their private quarters ('chamber'; l. 57), meanwhile sending the keys to their outer rooms and the chests in which they store their possessions to the Duchess. The reaction of the Officers will help add to the mood of the scene: questioning, uneasy, eager to please, or resentful. In some productions the first of a series of cries of pain from the Duchess in her quarters is heard. Bosola jeers at the Officers for their gullibility about the Switzer rumour, again reinforcing his intellectual superiority and calm.

68–84   Yet another short French scene, as the Officers exit to their quarters, leaving Antonio alone with Delio. Both are intensely concerned for the Duchess, and Antonio afraid for himself. He urges Delio to ride urgently to Rome on unspecified life-and-death business, further heightening the sense of danger surrounding the Duchess and Antonio. As at the end of the previous scene, Delio needs to calm the fearful Antonio, which he does by saying that his fears are, like belief in superstitions, entirely imaginary. As Delio swears to be a faithful friend, his sententious rhyming couplet will seem to signal the end of the scene, and perhaps Antonio is starting to exit back to the door that by now will be clearly thought of as towards the Duchess's chamber (Delio having left in another direction to take horse), when he is interrupted by the entry of Cariola.

85 to the end   Cariola need not enter 'with a Child' as in Quarto 4 (1708), although often she does. What is more important is the reinforcement by her entry and exit of the door towards the Duchess's chamber, which will be crucial in the next scene. Antonio seems to draw new energy from Cariola's news, and his determination to establish his newly born son's horoscope would not be unusual at the time, although for a modern audience it may seem related to the superstitions Delio has just been deriding. An atmosphere of complete trust is often evident between Cariola and Antonio, even as they exit in opposite directions.

Act II, scene iii

1–9   Structurally and visually Bosola's solo entry repeats the start of II.ii, intensified by the events of that scene and by his carrying a dark lantern (having a movable solid panel to hide the light when desired, and therefore useful to an eavesdropper or spy); on the fully lit early modern stage, it would be a signifier of darkness as well. If it really is 'very cold' (l. 19), Bosola's clothing may indicate this; perhaps he is dressed for outdoors. Presumably the 'shriek' (of labour) he hears as he enters, repeated at l. 6, is identified by the audience too as coming from the direction already identified as the Duchess's lodgings. Although the birth has already been announced at the end of II.ii, Webster seems to be employing a chronological overlap here in order to expand the confusion and danger surrounding the Duchess's giving birth. The night sounds and Bosola's jittery uncertainty recall *Macbeth*, II.ii.14–17.

9–52   When Antonio enters, Bosola identifies him before he speaks, but Antonio cannot see Bosola. Bosola may open his lantern so the light falls on Antonio. Once again, Antonio's fear is evident, and reinforced when he discovers Bosola present. Antonio's refusal to investigate the noise from the Duchess's lodgings (the direction he has probably just come from) seems to raise Bosola's suspicions; and

when Antonio starts questioning and accusing him, Bosola responds
with an insolent joke about saying his prayers, and then with an
obscene 'Spanish fig' gesture (l. 31) and fearless counter-threats.

This confrontation is interrupted by Antonio's nosebleed. 'Bleeding
at nose' was listed by Delio at II.ii.79 as an omen for the superstitious,
and Antonio seems upset by it. Crucially for the plot, he pulls a
handkerchief from his pocket, and this is usually why the horoscope
falls. He then threatens Bosola with house arrest by morning, and
forbids him from passing 'this door', presumably the one leading to
the 'Duchess' lodgings' (ll. 48, 50). Antonio's rhyming couplet to the
audience before he exits is another *sentia* ('sentence'; see pp. 13–14),
and may recall what the Duchess said at I.i.441–8 about the devious-
ness required to keep matters secret.

53 to the end   Bosola opens the dark lantern (his 'false friend';
l. 54) to signify that he is searching in darkness, then comments
to the audience on each increasingly relevant discovery about the
horoscope. The actor has to decide how much comedy to allow. The
more he plays, the better the audience may like him as a performer;
but there is a danger in playing the coincidences too much for laughs
('that's this year – that's this night – that's our Duchess'; ll. 56–9),
since it may suggest the actor is mocking the play. Bosola is sometimes criticized by realist critics for being slow on the uptake (for
example, in failing to deduce that Antonio is not the Duchess's pimp:
'If one could find the father now!' (l. 71) can hardly fail to draw a
laugh, when he is so close to the truth and gets it so wrong. But the
seriousness of his purpose, and the danger posed to the Duchess and
Antonio by the letter he will send to her brothers, are real, and best
not lost entirely in comedy. He, like Antonio, exits with a *sentia* that
clearly comments on what he has discovered about the Duchess in
this scene; and although neither he nor the audience will know it yet,
it will also turn out to be applicable to Julia in the next scene.

Act II, scene iv

1 to the end   *The scene is in two parts: first Julia's position as the Cardinal's
mistress is seen to be somewhat tense, then the second half reveals the arrival in
Rome of Bosola's letter to the Aragonian brothers, and shows Delio trying to
purchase her favours.*

1–39   'Sit' says the Cardinal the moment he enters with Julia. She may take one of the stools usually available on the Jacobean stage, but if the recollection of Orazio Busino is correct, he will command his 'harlot on his knee' (see pp. 91–2). If so, the stage tableau is scandalous, and emphasizes the corruption of this prince of the Catholic Church first recounted at I.i.153–66. This may be emphasized in modern productions by an elaborate set change as we move to Rome. Julia too is 'a witty false one' (l. 5), and if the audience picks up the repetition of '*witty*' from the final line of the scene just ended, they may also recall the masque of lust Bosola referred to in that *sententia*. Furthermore, much of the Cardinal's misogynistic dialogue now is about the inconstancy of women; a Renaissance commonplace, but seemingly placed here either for comparison or contrast with the admirable constancy we have so far seen from the Duchess. Julia cries, but the actress must decide whether Julia is genuinely upset, or is using her courtesan's tricks to manipulate the Cardinal out of his bullying mockery. He appears to gentle her out of her despondency, asking for kisses but still reminding her of her debt to him. This section of the scene can be played as a quiet or emotional lovers' tiff; as one-sided or mutual teasing; as cold criticism by the Cardinal; or, as in a number of modern productions, it can be fiercely or even sadistically erotic. Julia can be played as victim of a callous and powerful man, or as herself a skilful and controlling courtesan who gets what she wants despite the constraints on women at court.

39 to the end   A Servant enters to announce the arrival in Rome of a gentleman visitor for Julia as well as her husband, both of whom have ridden hard ('post', ll. 42, 45). The Cardinal leaves. Probably the Servant does too once he has ushered Delio into Julia's presence. In the early productions Delio was probably still wearing his riding boots, spurs, and cape.

Delio's visit to a woman we now know to be the Cardinal's mistress, especially given his flirtatious language, and his mockery of her husband Castruchio (whose very name suggests castration) as a cuckold, sits oddly with a man who up to now has seemed a reliable and steadfast friend of Antonio's who shares his dislike of the corruptness of the court and of great men. The audience will be further intrigued and perhaps unsettled when Delio offers Julia money. Even a small bag of gold is heavy, and the language suggests

that Delio shows it to her and handles it so as to 'Try the sound on't'
(l. 63; and cf. Ferdinand's suborning of Bosola in Act I). For the actor
of Delio, there is a clear choice whether to be more sexually flirtatious or more businesslike in what is clarified, following the brief
return of the Servant, as an offer to keep her as a paid courtesan.
This is in marked contrast to the wooing scene between the Duchess
and Antonio. Julia's responses to Delio – first a cool disparagement
(unless contradicted by kisses or caresses) of the proffered gold, then
an urgent offer that he should quickly state what he wants while they
are private, and finally her extraordinary exit line (which always gets
her a big laugh) that she'll ask her husband if she may – all these leave
Delio understandably confused about her intentions. 'Is this her wit
or honesty' he asks (l. 77), where 'wit' again echoes Bosola's *sententia*
at the end of the previous scene.

She may emphasize one kind of wit by throwing a wanton glance
at Delio as she leaves, or by taking the gold. This always raises a laugh,
but does little to support Delio's uncertainty. We may also wonder
whether Delio has an unrevealed motive.

The Servant's report that Bosola's letter has driven Ferdinand 'out
of his wits' (l. 69) leads Delio to conclude (correctly) that 'Antonio is
betrayed' (l. 80). Delio's comment to the audience about Antonio's
ambition does not match what Antonio said in I.i, but serves to
remind us again (as does the sententious final couplet) of the inherent
danger of crossing class boundaries, especially in secret.

Act II, scene v

1 to the end   The primary dynamic of this scene is established
from the moment of entry, with Ferdinand, enraged by the news
from Malfi, observed and questioned by the calmer Cardinal (who
probably enters second). A lot of information is given, especially
in the Cardinal's dialogue, about Ferdinand's acting, and of course
he enters clutching the letter from Bosola about the discovery of
the horoscope of the Duchess's apparently bastard child. Having
probably given his brother the letter at 'Read there' (l. 3), he needs
to snatch it back at 'Here's the cursèd day' (the horoscope gives the
'day' of birth) prior to gesturing at head or heart for the second 'here'
where the memory will 'stick' (ll. 14–15). Ferdinand is 'choleric' in
Renaissance humours theory/psychology (even calling for 'rhubarb'

(l. 12) to purge his choler), whereas the Cardinal is 'phlegmatic'. Ferdinand himself announces that he is 'grown mad' with the news, and the Cardinal sarcastically asks what 'prodigy' (l. 2) could have aroused him so, before urging him to stop shouting (a reminder of the pervasive presence of intelligencers). In addition to 'intemperate noise' (l. 51), Ferdinand's frenzy appears to drive him to constant movement about the stage (cf. 'tempest', l. 17; 'whirlwinds', l. 51) and shaking with rage ('palsy', l. 55; see also p. 127). At ll. 27–8 he either cries or pretends to do so, and the Cardinal, after failing to persuade him to 'be angry / Without this rupture' (ll. 55–6), describes him as 'stark mad' (l. 66) and threatens to leave altogether before Ferdinand finally calms down.

Both brothers are outraged at their sister having dishonoured their family by having an illegitimate child. But whereas the Cardinal's sense of their 'royal blood' being 'attainted' (ll. 22–3) is the legal sense of 'lineage' being 'stained or corrupted', Ferdinand responds as if his sister's actual blood were 'infected with contagion' that needs an extreme medical response. His reaction throughout is to her specific and physical actions, to her body, to 'see her in the shameful act of sin' (l. 41). His imagery for her, and for the men who may serve her lust, seems obsessively concerned with her sexuality, and since the mid twentieth century a Freudian interpretation of incestuous desire has influenced a number of actors of Ferdinand (Simon Russell Beale at Greenwich in 1995 was visibly aroused and disturbed). This can be overtly manifested at various other points in the play as well, especially with the discussion about the poniard at I.i.330–40, and in III.ii. Actors who have made this strand of Ferdinand's character subconscious rather than understood have often succeeded better at conveying the complexity of the brothers' Spanish concern with honour and pride of family, and with the real lycanthropia that will develop from the nascent madness of Ferdinand (sometimes foreshadowed in this scene). Furthermore, the images of storm and fire that reach their culmination at ll. 66–70 traditionally refer not just to choler, and to sexual desire (here incestuous), but also to witchcraft, hell, and the devil in the most serious religious terms. Ferdinand would act so that the Duchess may not 'ascend to heaven' (l. 68).

The Cardinal's avoidance of 'intemperate anger' (l. 58) is chilling in the circumstances, and far from the audience perceiving him as a moderating or generous influence, is likely to see only confirmation of Antonio's characterization of him at I.i.156–66 as a dangerous schemer associated with 'the devil' (I.i.186). It is not clear whether his reaction 'Are you stark mad?' (l. 66) is to Ferdinand's specific threat to kill their sister, or to the suggestion that all three of them deserve death for a shared sin. When the Cardinal eventually calms his brother, Ferdinand also appears a dangerous watcher, determined not to act until he learns who the man is who has dishonoured and 'leaps' their sister. Then, he promises, he will act with ferocity.

Whereas Act I ended with the glow of a successful romantic attachment between the Duchess and Antonio (despite Cariola's caveat), Act II now ends with betrayal of their secret and the threat of dire revenge.

Act III

Act III, scene i

1–57   Candles or torches may be brought on stage to indicate night. Delio may again be wearing boots, spurs, and riding cloak as just arrived, as may Ferdinand later in the scene. The passage of at least two years (time enough for the Duchess to have two more children) is assisted structurally by the act break and music in the early performances, and is made specific by Antonio's welcome to Delio after so long away (a reversal of the opening of I.i, but symmetrical as these two close friends open what can be regarded as the second half of the play). Self-consciousness about theatrical conventions appears to be foregrounded as Delio says he can imagine he has seen the Duchess within the last half hour. This can be played as an effective metatheatrical joke. Clearly Webster does not want his audience to be lulled into an undemanding acceptance of simple narrative realism; he continually provides images and words that require analysis and thought.

Delio is anxious to find out if the Cardinal knows of the Duchess's children, but Antonio is more concerned about the presence of Ferdinand at the Duchess's court. His language recalls the vocabulary of II.v: Ferdinand's 'quiet' in place of the 'tempest', his apparent 'sleep', seem devilish in their danger (ll. 21–4).

Delio takes it for granted that the Duchess's children cannot have been kept a secret, and asks about two kinds of popular opinion, that of the commoners, and that of the 'graver heads, / Which would be politic' (ll. 26–7). Antonio's response is instructive, but his tone is less easy to ascertain.

37–57 Ferdinand and the Duchess certainly enter at this point. The actors of Silvio, Roderigo, and Grisolan would all be available if a crowded court scene is wanted, which might be appropriate if Ferdinand's purpose is to use a court occasion to put the Duchess off-balance. More important still, Bosola, as Ferdinand's intelligencer at her court, is certainly on stage by l. 57. However, his name is only listed at the head of the scene in the massed stage direction (see pp. 9–10), so precisely when he enters is uncertain. Some editors have him enter at l. 57, on the basis that his entry will cross the Duchess's exit, and thus visually underline Ferdinand's hypocrisy; but other editors have Bosola enter now with Ferdinand, which has the drama-turgical advantage that Ferdinand's spy can assist him to observe the reaction of the Duchess, and of Antonio. We might compare Hamlet asking Horatio to observe Claudius during the 'Mousetrap' scene in *Hamlet* (III.ii).

Either way, Ferdinand is notable for sudden shifts of topic and interest. He does not press the Duchess about Count Malateste as a chosen husband: has he lost interest, or is he deliberately confusing her? His greeting to Antonio (whom he believes to be his sister's pander) is likely to worry both Antonio and the Duchess. She certainly brings Ferdinand's attention back to her as she starts to raise the question of a 'scandalous report', an adroit political ploy to counter the rumours. But her obvious relief when Ferdinand says he wouldn't care even if the rumours were true is clear to Ferdinand (and to Bosola if he is present); the moment she and the rest of the court have left he confirms that he has all the evidence he needs ('Her guilt treads on / Hot-burning coulters', ll. 56–7).

57–93 This section, as so often when Ferdinand is central, changes direction several times. And, as before, Ferdinand's shifting attention may induce caution, tension, or aggression in Bosola. Initially the dialogue seems to be plot-driven: Ferdinand wants to know what further information has been gleaned. But Bosola's throwaway reply, that the answer is in the stars, leads into a surprisingly long digression about astrology and sorcery. Bosola says he believes in sorcery and witchcraft. Such beliefs were widespread at the time the play was written, but the audience may be surprised to find this chink in Bosola's usual cynicism. Ferdinand, however, is obsessed with the Duchess. In a rising tide of anger, partly directed at Bosola, he seems as out of control as in II.v, declaring that 'The witchcraft lies in her rank blood' (l. 78).

His determination to force a confession from her returns him to the intrigue, demanding if Bosola has the duplicate key to her bedchamber that he has recently acquired. The key is an important prop here, as the audience sees it passed to Ferdinand. Whereas Bosola at I.i.256 implied but did not ask Ferdinand to explain himself, here he does, and Ferdinand's quick reply can be funny as well as unsettling. In part Ferdinand seems to be reminding Bosola of his lower status, in part fantasizing about his own abilities. In both cases Bosola's rude reply holds shock value: how will Ferdinand respond? The demand for Bosola's hand may be utterly unpredictable. Will he shake it (which the offer implies, and, slightly surprisingly, actually happens)? Will he pull Bosola close enough to bury a knife in him (as seems almost equally possible)? Will he read his palm?

By this stage of the play Ferdinand has become dangerously volatile. Scene-ending *sententiae* in rhyming couplets like ll. 92–3 tend to reflect not just the character, but also the view of the playwright himself (see pp. 13–14); in this case, if Ferdinand really is grateful for having his faults pointed out, the audience may well be very surprised or suspicious. Although the text prints '*Exeunt*' following the final couplet, Ferdinand's 'Farewell' to Bosola at l. 91 may indicate that Bosola is to exit at that point, which would reinforce a likelihood of Ferdinand's couplet, spoken direct to the audience, being without irony.

Act III, scene ii

1 to the end   *This long scene almost contains the play in miniature. The first French scene within it displays the loving domesticity of the Duchess and Antonio, followed by the reversal of her good fortune in the following long French scene of Ferdinand's entry and threats to her; then follow several short French scenes leading to the flight of Antonio and the Duchess's disastrous* *trust in Bosola. By the end of III.ii the Duchess and Antonio are in crisis, and Ferdinand's revenge has now found out its second target: his sister's lover.*

1–57 Even stripped to its simplest requirements, this first French scene is peaceful and domestic: the Duchess preparing for bed, Cariola in attendance, and Antonio at ease and joking with both. Candles or torches may indicate night. Often in modern productions a bed is on stage, and the lighting is usually warm in colour. Sometimes, however, the threat of what is to come is signalled by stark design, or ambiguous grills or shadows over the bed. Antonio may be provided with a secret entrance. Sometimes evidence of children is seen, such as a rocking horse, or dolls, suggesting happy marriage.

The instruction to Cariola to bring the casket for her jewellery, and a looking glass, may mean Cariola has to exit, returning in time to hear l. 10. Despite the relaxed tone of the dialogue, the Duchess is aware of the danger while Ferdinand is at court; hence her decision that Antonio must not stay with her this night. The mock-servility of Antonio removing his hat and kneeling to her ('cap and knee', l. 5) initiates a relaxed, intimate, and witty conversation between them, in which the trusted Cariola joins in fully. They share sexual jokes ('lodging', ll. 2, 6; 'use', l. 9; 'sleep', ll. 9, 10; 'lie', ll. 11, 17) about Antonio's secret appearance 'only in the night' (l. 8), another reminder of the deception on which this secret marriage is based. The two kisses draw Antonio and the Duchess into physical proximity (if they weren't already), and skilfully allow Antonio to turn his teasing attention to Cariola. Her 'Never' (l. 23) in response to when she will marry can be played as critical or foreboding (cf. the final speech of Act I, and ll. 316–21 later in this scene), but more often is her laughingly teasing Antonio in turn. Usually all three of them are laughing by the end of Antonio's description of the three goddesses 'stark naked' (l. 40).

Antonio's continued teasing of both the women as ugly ('hard-favoured', l. 45) reinforces our sense of his real love for the Duchess and fondness for Cariola. The Duchess's 'merry' (l. 53) response leads into the transition to the next French scene: she becomes distracted by a tangle in her hair (symbolic?), so even if Cariola was brushing it earlier, the Duchess herself seems to be now. She may pick up the mirror to examine it more closely, thus providing a realistic opportunity for Antonio and Cariola to tease her further before leaving while she is still talking to them.

58–71 As the Duchess continues talking (as she thinks) to Antonio and Cariola, Ferdinand enters; but just when is uncertain. He must be on stage by the time the Duchess sees him at l. 69. He may enter after l. 61 as in Q4; but that placing reflects no more than theatre practice nearly a hundred years after the first performances. He may enter one line later, after l. 62, as many modern editors choose, since that allows Ferdinand's entry to coincide with the Duchess's warning about the danger from 'my brothers'. The Arden edition places the entry earlier, after l. 60, allowing Ferdinand to be on stage as she says 'You have cause to love me'; whether or not Ferdinand briefly thinks it is addressed to him, the audience may be led to think of the dissonance of the line with the entry, and Ferdinand's 'wilful' (l. 118) obsession with her. Presumably the Duchess is seated well forward on the stage, facing away from both where Antonio and Cariola exited, and Ferdinand's entrance point. The menace of his listening to her as she teases her love (Antonio), warns him not to sleep with her, and expresses her desire to reconcile her brothers, is heightened if Ferdinand is carrying the '*poniard*' that he will give her at l. 71, since his intention will appear to be murder. And if she is already undressed for bed, she will appear that much more vulnerable.

The staging of her discovery of his presence, and the giving of the poniard, also offer various choices. The line to Antonio 'Have you lost your tongue?' (l. 68) is the obvious cue for her to look for him. She may then turn and see Ferdinand, or she may see him the mirror with which she has been examining the colour of her hair. ''Tis welcome' (l. 69) is most likely a reaction to his discovery of her secret marriage; as she says in the next line, at least she will now know her fate. It has sometimes been played as a reaction to seeing the poniard, but Ferdinand's response 'Die then, quickly!' (l. 71) seems to match gesture to words perfectly if it is only seen by the Duchess at that moment. The manner of its giving is also subject to acting choice: options have included ceremoniously, casually, viciously, blade first, hilt first, hilt forming a cross, phallic suggestiveness, and mirroring the manner of handling it at I.i.330–32. Whichever choices are made, this is an intense moment of crisis.

72–141 Ferdinand now dominates the Duchess and the scene. Initially he hardly speaks to her, instead invoking the abstractions 'Virtue' (l. 72) and Reason. Not only is he enraged, he seems almost beyond reason. We may see a combination of rage and incest, with Ferdinand sexually seizing his sister, or throwing her on the bed. The Duchess tries to explain reasonably (albeit in great fear) that she is married, though 'Happily [i.e., haply, perhaps] not to your liking' (l. 83), and offers to introduce her husband. She evidently thinks Antonio arranged for Ferdinand to gain entrance. Ferdinand demands her silence, claiming – significantly given the frequent acting choice to allow Ferdinand's developing lycanthropia to be glimpsed – that she creates a noise worse than a wolf's howling. Turning his attention to the absent man ('Whate'er thou art', l. 90) whom he takes to be his sister's lover, Ferdinand may well range the stage as he did in II.v, and in this case hurl his words at stage hangings, doors, or in other ways offstage, since he is sure the man can hear him. The actor has powerful language and ideas to work with, not least the reversal of his decision to discover his sister's lover, which he now fears to do because the 'violent effects' might 'damn us both' (ll. 94–5). A visceral fear of his own instincts and possible actions, a fear of his own personality and desires, constitutes a recognition, albeit imperfect, of both his own destructive urges and his excessive interest in his sister's sexuality.

His warning to the Duchess to keep her 'lecher' (l. 100) hidden employs bestial imagery: 'dogs and monkeys' may recall 'goats and monkeys' in *Othello* (IV.i.265). Her demand of him starting, 'Why might not I marry' (l. 109) has on occasion been played as strongly feminist, but the rhythmic structure of the verse here suggests that Webster intended her to be far from assertive, whereas Ferdinand's reply sounds like a funeral drum (see pp. 14–15).

When she claims that 'my reputation / Is safe' (ll. 118–19), which the audience knows to be untrue, Ferdinand responds with a long set-piece parable about 'Reputation, Love, and Death' (l. 122). It is structurally and dramaturgically similar to the Duchess's tale of the Salmon that will come at the end of III.v, in that although both speeches fit perfectly well with what the characters wish to say at that point, they are both distinct in style from the rest of the dialogue. They are perhaps best compared to arias in an opera: reiteration and expansion of crucial thematic and emotional elements that need fuller expression. The moral of this 'sad tale' (III.v.124) is simple: reputation, once lost, can never be recovered. Although realist productions often cut part or all of the speech, it can be theatrically effective: in the Manchester Royal Exchange production, Ferdinand cast himself as Reputation, holding up the poniard as Death, and a child's doll (see commentary on ll. 1–57 above) as Love. At 'and so for you' he gave her the dagger, at the first 'I will never see you more' he dropped the doll, and at 'witches' he crushed the doll's head under his foot (ll. 133–41). The repetition of 'I will never see you more' at l. 141 will reinforce his use of the emphatic 'will' rather than the grammatically neutral 'shall', and allows the actor to explore the character's motive for being so determined: is his exit line a threat against her, or an attempt to protect her from himself?

142–160   Antonio may burst on stage as if only now armed '*with a pistol*', and ready for confrontation with Ferdinand; or he may enter more fearfully (peering around a curtain or door first to see if the coast is clear), having heard but not intervened, which might better match what we have seen of his character so far. The threat against Cariola confirms his inability to take real action, and he again seems paralysed by events when knocking is heard.

Probably Cariola goes to the door as Antonio and the Duchess stand distraught. When Cariola announces it is Bosola, the Duchess takes a moment to acknowledge again the strange way that secrecy and intrigue have led them into a mire, as if their marriage were 'unjust' (l. 158) rather than virtuous. Nevertheless, she now shows her mettle as she reveals she has a plan ready for Antonio to escape.

161–73   Cariola usually controls the action at the start, waiting till Antonio has slipped out before opening the door to Bosola. He walks into a situation full of tension, but does not yet know what has happened, apart from Ferdinand's 'whirlwind' departure saying the Duchess is 'undone' (ll. 161, 164). Therefore he too is on full alert, but must appear not to know anything other than what he reports Ferdinand as saying. The actor playing the Duchess must decide whether her story about Antonio and loan fraud is carefully rehearsed or made up on the spot, and if the excessive circumstantial detail should make it obvious to Bosola that she is lying. Either way, Bosola reveals to the audience that he is not persuaded ('This is cunning', l. 171).

174–81   Webster's choice to alternate short French scenes is evident here. He could easily have placed these quick instructions from

the Duchess about hiding in Ancona after l. 160, just before Bosola
entered. The rapid pace of exit and entrance builds the sense of a
crisis unfolding at speed as she hears Bosola returning with the
Officers; and it provides a transparent contrast for the audience
between the reality of the Duchess's love and care for Antonio here
and the smokescreen she will deploy in a moment.

182–209   A strange unreality pervades this brief French scene, since
the audience knows it is a charade. They also recognize the credu-
lous Officers from II.ii, and will expect little but low comedy from
them. Attention is therefore on Bosola's observation, and on how
the Duchess will attempt to protect Antonio. He gives her a cue with
his first line, 'Will your grace hear me?' (l. 182), as if he were pleading
his innocence. But is this a mark of his intelligence, or again an indication that he is bereft of ideas in a crisis, and has to rely on her to
take the initiative? Her accusations in this little 'play-within-a-play'
sound controlled and reasoned, as do Antonio's responses to her
and to Bosola and the Officers. There are, however, two other kinds
of discourse going on. First, Antonio's bitterness about 'the incon-
stant / And rotten ground of service', although part of his pretence of
pleading his case, sounds also like a real attack on court corruption.
Second, and more important, both the Duchess and Antonio embed
coded messages of love within their apparent anger: 'I have got well
by you', 'your *quietus*' (cf. I.i.464), 'h'as done that you would not think
of'; and from Antonio, 'I am all yours', 'serve … with body, and soul'
(ll. 184, 186, 191, 206, 208–9). As Antonio moves to exit, probably
having given up his chain of office, the Duchess and the audience will
usually be keeping an eye on Bosola to see if he will make any move
to seize Antonio. The Duchess has already had to stop the Officers
once at l. 190 ('let him [go]').

210–28   With Antonio gone, the Officers respond to the Duchess's
question about him with predicably bizarre and extravagant criticism, in tune with their foolish rumour-mongering in II.ii. Thus,
this French scene is in part grotesque comedy that satirizes the
credulity of the Officers, and in part satire on their sycophantic will-
ingness to criticize someone out of favour, 'where this man's head
lies at that man's foot' (I.i.67). In addition, the scene confirms how
easily 'Reputation' (l. 122) is lost. Bosola will of course be observing

closely how the Duchess responds to this criticism; possibly her curt dismissal of them ('Leave us", l. 228) is because she cannot stand to listen to them a moment longer. Her reaction may determine what Bosola's tactics will now be.

229–76   With the Officers gone, Bosola, in three long speeches, first dismisses them as 'flatt'ring rogues' (l.239) in his typical malcontent manner, then dangles bait in front of the Duchess by sighing out 'Alas, poor gentleman' (l. 243). She plays devil's advocate here and at l. 261, but probably to encourage him; she may cry as she hears Bosola's praise of Antonio. There is a fundamental question about Bosola's motivation, and sometimes the scene is heavily cut so as to bypass the complexity. Put simply, how much, if any, of what Bosola is saying about Antonio does he believe? Is his elaborate hyperbole about the Duchess's favourite entirely to lure her into giving herself away; or is there either open admiration for Antonio, or a suppressed admission despite himself of his rival's virtues that refuses to stay hidden even as he tries to entrap the Duchess? Not only does Bosola repeat his own and Antonio's criticism in Act I of corrupt aristocrats and rulers, but his pungent language (such as the grotesquely striking image of the rottenness of politicians and spies at ll. 269–72) probably justifies an element of emotional sincerity in what is probably a carefully hypocritical speech designed to elicit the real feelings of the Duchess (but see p. 126).

277–325   As the Duchess starts to reveal her true feelings to Bosola with 'you render me excellent music' (l. 277), Cariola will sometimes take a pace towards the Duchess, more suspicious of him than her mistress. With simple sincere language ('This good one that you speak of is my husband', l. 278) that is in sharp contrast with Bosola's laboured phrases, she takes Bosola into her confidence. His response praises both Antonio and the Duchess in ways she wants to hear, and thereby encourage her to confide further in him. At the same time, his praise is satiric criticism of courtly norms, and thus suits his malcontent mode of court railing, and indeed is probably close to his own view. His praise of both her and Antonio is so inflated, however, that sometimes in performance the Duchess's demand for 'concealment' (l. 303) of what she has said seems to derive from a momentary (and short-lived) doubt as to whether he can be trusted. His pledge of secrecy (at the RSC in 1989 he knelt in fealty) persuades her.

She immediately takes him into her confidence about joining Antonio in Ancona, and assigns him the task of conveying 'all my coin and jewels' (l. 306) to them. His instant agreement, and what appears a thoughtful improvement of the plan – that she should pretend a pilgrimage to the shrine of Loretto, near Ancona – may serve several purposes. He will gain her trust; he will seize control of all her portable wealth; and her false use of religion (cf. III.iii.60–62) to hide her flight is likely to discredit her. Cariola objects to the 'jesting with religion' (l. 320). Whether she does so from religious belief, or from suspicion of Bosola, is for the actor to decide, but the response of the Duchess suggests that religious belief is certainly possible. The Duchess's exit lines are again a sententious rhyming couplet that seems to encapsulate the disaster that has befallen her during the course of this long scene that started with domestic love and harmony, and is ending with frantically improvised flight; yet its regular rhythm and predictable rhyme, as well as its balanced moderation of language, argues her fortitude in the face of disaster.

326 to the end   Admitting to the audience that he is a 'politician' (l. 326; in Webster's time it meant a schemer or plotter), Bosola acknowledges that he is doing the devil's work. He despises himself, but has no choice but to report it all to Ferdinand. However, he nearly always gains audience sympathy at this point: first for his honest self-knowledge of his 'base quality' (l. 330), and secondly for the ironic humour he can bring to the closing *sententia*, in which he compares himself to an artist who is highly praised for his painting of '*weeds*' (l. 334), though they are not worthy of being painted at all.

Act III, scene iii

1–7   Two new aristocratic characters enter with the Cardinal, Ferdinand, and courtiers. One is a fop, carrying elaborate paper plans ('plot', l. 7) of military fortifications, wearing a lady's taffeta scarf, and probably sniffing its perfume just before l. 24, and is likely in the original performances to have been the same actor who played Castruchio early in the play; these features suggest he may appear to be a foolish figure of fun. His flattery of the Cardinal, who is about to 'turn soldier' (l. 1), includes a gesture to the other new character, possibly in costume suggesting an aristocratic soldier (such as a steel gorget), now identified as the Marquis of Pescara. Later described as 'a noble old fellow' (V.i.60), Pescara probably has a white beard. The presentation, perhaps self-importantly by the fop, of the plans (possibly requiring a large table on stage) draws everyone except Delio, Silvio, and – at least initially – Ferdinand together where they are not heard, but are observed and commented on in a way that may recall Delio and Antonio's commentary on court figures in Act I. This fundamentally changes the dynamic of the scene, despite it including all the same characters.

8–34   Ferdinand identifies the unknown fop as Count Malateste, the man the Duchess dismissed at III.i.42 as 'a stick of sugar candy', and Delio and Silvio's sardonic mockery of him reinforces the audience impression of him (and provides the actor with many pointers for performance). Although Ferdinand initiates this satire, he says nothing after l. 12 (his speech heading at l. 21 in the Revels Student Edition is an error; Q1 is clear that it is Silvio). He is likely to join the group looking at the plans, leaving Delio and Silvio to comment on the group, and what is evidently Malateste's attention-drawing presence. Despite the satiric comedy of the language, and probably of performance by Malateste, the development of war as an element in the play (cf. the brief reference to the 'leaguer', or camp, at I.i.221) is new and potentially serious.

35–59   The arrival of Bosola, probably booted and spurred, could be earlier than this point, but cannot be at the start of the scene, as he was present at the end of the preceding scene. It is best here, with as much imaginative time as possible to allow for his travel from Malfi to Rome, and probably wasting no time in interrupting the consultation and drawing Ferdinand and the Cardinal aside to tell them his news. The audience already know what he will be telling them (unlike everyone on stage). Pescara joins Delio and Silvio, and expresses what sounds like reasonable apprehension about the sudden disruption of their meeting by Bosola, and how great men are destructive in their power. Bosola is identified (no doubt during his mimed speech to Ferdinand and the Cardinal) as an ambitious scholar in the past (Ian McKellen played him in wire-rimmed glasses, a more textually-based choice than the frequent costuming as a soldier), and then the observation switches to the reactions of the two brothers. They will enact what the observers report seeing: signs of anger, violence, and haughty pride. Ferdinand's laughter is recognized as a danger sign, and Pescara shares Delio's anxiety about what is afoot. The 'deformed silence' (l. 58) that Delio observes may have followed Ferdinand's laugh, and may now provide the cue for Ferdinand, the Cardinal, and Bosola to come forward as everyone else moves apart.

60 to the end As earlier, the alternation of the two groups of actors creates almost new French scenes within the scene, with a new dynamic each time. The Cardinal is especially angry at the report that the Duchess is fleeing to Ancona under the guise of a religious pilgrimage (cf. Cariola's concern at III.ii.316–21). Ferdinand, typically, has more confused motives, that include seeing 'her fault and beauty' (l. 62) as a strangely attractive leprosy. They quickly agree on the first step to be taken against her: the Cardinal will have her banished from Ancona. Ferdinand says he will not attend (perhaps because of his declaration never to see her more), and his 'fare you well' indicates that the Cardinal probably exits at this point. Ferdinand instructs Bosola to write to the Duchess's son by her first husband to drive a wedge between him and his mother. This is the first the audience has heard of a young Duke of Malfi, whose existence demands that we work out that the Duchess must be ruling as regent until he comes of age. This means, of course, that the son she has had by Antonio will not inherit the Duchy. Because the implications of a previous son are difficult to convey (though not impossible) later in the play, and the young Duke is never mentioned again, ll. 69–71 are frequently cut in performance. Finally Ferdinand, after railing about Antonio's lack of aristocratic birth, orders Bosola to call out an armed force, presumably to capture his sister.

Act III, scene iv

1–7 The two men who now enter will be instantly identifiable as Pilgrims by their costume (see p. 5). The '*Shrine of our Lady of Loretto*' that they admire was famous in Europe for its black Madonna and child, a version of which may appear on stage on an altar. The Pilgrims serve as a chorus, reminding the audience that the Cardinal is to 'resign his cardinal's hat' (in order to become a soldier), and informing us that the Duchess will also be present 'To pay her vow of pilgrimage' (l. 6). A confrontation is imminent.

7.1–23 The audience has been led to expect a 'noble ceremony' (l. 7), and this '*dumb show*' (l. 7.6) can be spectacular in the theatre. The chaplain to the Venetian embassy in London seems to have attended one of the early performances: despite his disgust at what he took to be a Protestant intention to portray Catholicism in as bad a light as possible, he acknowledges the grandeur, formality, ceremonious-ness, and even 'panache' of the action described in the long stage direction here (see pp. 6 and 91–2). Certainly, the action of disrobing the Cardinal and then arming him will take some time, and require a number of attendants (at least three or four actors would have been available in the original company, and modern productions sometimes use more). In addition, it can be made clearly emblem-atic, as in the 1971 RSC production in which he was finally armed in total plate armour with visor down, so that the audience saw not the character, but the Church stripped of its disguising robes to be revealed as barbaric. In the same year at Stratford in Canada the chanting churchmen in swirling incense attending the Cardinal were wearing death's heads. It can be a nightmare vision. The nature of the Duchess's banishment is not specified, but she may well be kneeling (like a penitent; in this case refused forgiveness), and ll. 36–7 tell us that the Cardinal (no longer in church robes) wrenches the Duchess's wedding ring from her finger with great violence.

The entire dumb show is accompanied by music. Although the triumphalist martial words of the 'ditty' (marginal note oppo-site ll. 8–11) that Webster disclaimed are undistinguished, an early version of the printed text uses the work 'hymn', so clearly the theatre had understood the sense of '*very solemn music*' (l. 7.8). Sometimes the religious music turns into a threatening cacophony, entirely in keeping with what the Venetian chaplain thought the whole scene was intended to portray.

24 to the end The Pilgrims, chorus-like, comment on what they have seen. They seem like normative figures, surprised at the Duchess marrying beneath her, but critical of the cruelty of the Cardinal. Furthermore, they agree that there has been no justice in the seizing of her duchy or her banishment, only a display of the Cardinal's power to influence the Pope. Their sympathy for Antonio is not only choric in its generality, but looks forward to the next scene as well as commenting on the scene just ending.

Act III, scene v

1–*to the end* *Although often shortened or even cut altogether in perform-ance, this scene is emotionally powerful, full of pathos and foreboding. It offers reaction and reflection after the frantic action that has gone before, and a sorrowful counter-example to the domestic happiness with which Act III opened.*

1–21 As the Duchess and Antonio enter with their family and retinue they will be dressed for outdoors (the first outdoor scene in the play); Antonio may be booted and spurred, and the Duchess wearing a 'safeguard', an outer skirt to protect the dress when riding. Or perhaps they look like refugees, especially if the few male serv-ants are carrying bundles or travelling trunks. The oldest child, a boy, and the middle child, probably a girl, are present, and Cariola is carrying the baby ('thy sweet armful', l. 84). They may give signs of fatigue, sometimes clearly stopping for a brief rest before continuing. A servant may be put on guard or sent to scout, to indicate that the entire party is nervous.

'Banished Ancona!' (l.1) is a clear indication that the Duchess is still absorbing the implications of the action of III.iv. The tone of this section is elegiac, a lamentation for their fall in fortune. 'This puts me in mind of death', says the Duchess, and then makes a bitter joke about doctors. Her dream of pearls signifies weeping, says Antonio. No one does anything; they are simply coming to terms with their new situation.

22–55 Bosola's sudden arrival, no doubt booted and spurred, may provoke unease or fear in the children. He instantly presents a letter to the Duchess ('From my brother', she asks at l. 22), but she berates him for his treacherous behaviour before she starts reading it. She is also now suspicious enough to recognize the 'politic equivoca-tion' (l. 29) in the letter of Ferdinand's request for Antonio's '*head*' and '*heart*' (ll. 28, 35). She probably gives it back to Bosola, or throws it down, at a moment when the gesture can punctuate her speech (perhaps after 'riddles' at l. 41). Antonio, too, makes clear his distrust of Ferdinand and the Cardinal when Bosola seems to hold out the letter to him ('And what of this?', l. 48). Bosola is clearly the first of the 'Bloodhounds' who have been sent out to find them. Bosola's sneer at Antonio's low 'breeding' (l. 52) is no more than what he has done throughout the play, but it combines with the threat of 'You shall shortly hear from's' (l. 55). In the 1960 Stratford production the boy visibly relaxed only after Bosola had left.

56–92 The first five lines of this new French scene advance the plot: the Duchess, yet again in command, urges Antonio to take their 'eldest son' (l. 58) and flee to Milan, splitting the family to increase the chance of at least some of them surviving. The rest of the scene is a painful leave-taking, full of foreboding. Antonio is initially comforter, assuring the Duchess that things will improve (or, in the image of a celestial watchmaker, be mended), or reminding her of the proverbial and religious benefits of suffering. The Duchess, however, is more deeply pessimistic, not only envisioning their separation as being just as bad as 'To see you dead' (l. 67), but parting from her son pleased that he cannot understand the biblical linking of knowledge with sorrow (see ll. 67–71). She sees God's 'heavy hand' (l. 78) in their suffering. The pathos of the scene is increased as Antonio takes leave of Cariola and the baby, and he embraces the Duchess as his final act before leaving. She senses that his speech 'Came from a dying father' (l. 88), in a speech that is deeply moving in the theatre if the relationship between the two has been thoroughly developed in the play, a moment of deep tenderness even as the family is being torn apart. Antonio exits to 'danger' (l. 92) with their elder son, and the Duchess says, simply, 'My laurel is all withered' (l. 93): an image of an evergreen wreath of triumph dying, and an evil omen (see *Richard II*, II.iv.7–8). The aptness of what she has said is confirmed by Cariola's sighting of soldiers approaching.

93 to the end The 'armèd men' (l. 94) are called both 'Soldiers' and 'a Guard' at different parts of Q1; and if they are soldiers, it is entirely possible they enter in orderly ranks to the 'thunder' (l. 100) of a drum. In modern productions they often appear suddenly and surround the Duchess, Cariola, and the children (and the servants if they have not already fled, or do not flee now) at gunpoint. The opening stage direction says the soldiers are wearing '*vizards*' (i.e., vizors, which mask their faces), but is ambiguous about whether Bosola is; the Duchess's line about beating in Bosola's 'counterfeit face' (l. 118) tends to support the theory that he is masking his face too, though it is possible she is simply referring to his treachery as making him a 'counterfeit'. Bosola will need to decide whether, and if so why, he intends to disguise his face and perhaps his voice from her; if he does, he will still want the audience to know who he is, and will have to find a way to do so. For the soldiers to be vizored makes them an anonymous force. Quite apart from the theatrical advantage of hiding from the audience the busy extras who have most recently been playing '*divers* Churchmen' (III.iv.7.9) and Pilgrims, their faceless, armed and threatening presence will be unnerving for the Duchess.

This is the second time in the play she has calmly said 'welcome' to apparent death (l. 95, and III.ii.69). She demonstrates what the play continually regards as the greatness of character inherent in a true prince, and at the same time the acceptance of oppression that so many references in the play have put into a biblical or religious context. Bosola finds her weak point, however, when he says 'you must see your husband no more' (l. 99). Her 'misery' (l. 105) becomes more apparent, even as she sardonically notes that being imprisoned in her palace probably means death. She says neither child is old enough to talk (presumably to suggest they are no danger; we find out at IV.ii.204 what should already be apparent from the age of the young performer, that she is old enough to 'Say her prayers'), but Bosola's sneer at Antonio as a 'base, low fellow' enrages the Duchess. But she controls herself, and starts the fable of the Salmon.

Like Ferdinand's story of Reputation in III.ii, this 'Sad tale' (l. 124) is clearly allegorical, and equally clearly Christian in its intent. The Roman god Jupiter represents God, the 'fisher' (l. 137) Christ, the 'market' (l. 138) the day of judgement, and the 'cook and fire' (l. 139) certainly the devil and hell. She is speaking of humility, and true value as opposed to merely the high place one may occupy. Indeed, the final couplet includes a *sententia* that encapsulates the fable in one line: '*There's no deep valley but near some great hill*' (l. 144); Webster elsewhere refers to mountains as 'deformed heaps', and valleys 'wholesomer' (see also Isaiah 40: 4). Alternatively, a modern audience may prefer to understand the final couplet as suggesting that however low one is driven by 'the oppressor's will' (l. 143), high aspiration will continue to be a virtue. And so the Duchess, Cariola, and the two younger children are led off under armed guard.

Act IV

Act IV, scene i

1–17   The pause and music in early production between the acts will imply some passage of time since the arrest of the Duchess at the end of Act III. Lighting is very important in this scene, so servants with torches probably enter with Ferdinand and Bosola. On the Globe stage torches would make almost no difference to actual light, and at the Blackfriars not very much; but their presence or absence was a convention the audience understood, just as modern stage lighting can allow an audience to see characters dimly or intermittently, but be understood to be so 'dark' that they cannot see each other. Bosola's description to Ferdinand of the Duchess behaving 'Nobly' (l. 2) in her imprisonment will not only prepare us for seeing the Duchess bearing her adversity well, but also alerts us to Bosola's apparent admiration (and sympathy?) for her. The report infuriates Ferdinand, who demands Bosola convey 'what I told you' (l. 17). Possibly he hears the Duchess approaching, or sees additional servants with torches entering.

18–28   Presumably Ferdinand's torch-bearers remain on stage, and more may enter with the Duchess and Cariola. Her costume, demeanour, even makeup, may be significantly different from when we last saw her, registering possibly some rigours of imprisonment, and the 'behaviour' (l. 5) described by Bosola, including possibly evidence of her 'tears' (l. 8), and her 'strange disdain' (l. 12). Bosola's emollient message that Ferdinand will visit her in the dark and be reconciled leads her to instruct the servants to 'Take hence the lights' (l. 28), leaving her, and presumably Cariola and Bosola, in the 'dark' (see note above).

29–53   Although in modern production this grisly French scene usually takes place in darkness that in some cases is almost total, the play was written for theatres in which stage and audience shared the same light throughout (see p. 7). 'This darkness' (l. 30) was therefore largely imaginary, a convention accepted by actors and audience. The Duchess begs her brother's pardon, and he gives it, but almost immediately makes it clear that his hatred remains, as he refuses to recognize her as married or her children as legitimate. He tells her, however, that his purpose is reconciliation, and offers her what she, in the 'darkness', assumes is his hand. The audience in early, and most modern, productions will see (at a moment to be decided by the actor of Ferdinand) that it is not his, but a separate '*dead man's hand*' (l. 43.1). Thus audience attention is not on melodramatic sudden horror, but on the language and action of the Duchess. Presumably she has knelt, and kisses the hand and what she thinks is her brother's ring (his 'love token', l. 47). If Ferdinand takes a step back here, the audience sees the horrific trick he is playing. She feels that it is 'very cold' (l.51), and is solicitous for his health. Her exclamation 'Hah!' (l. 53) often follows her running her hand up the wrist and finding it unconnected to an arm, but unable to believe it. The audience can see her, but she can 'see' neither the hand nor Ferdinand. She calls for 'Lights!', which may be brought on stage quickly enough that 'O, horrible!' is spoken when she can see that she is holding, or has dropped, or hurled away: a dead man's hand. Ferdinand exits while she is still focused on the hand.

54–110   The Duchess is allowed almost no time to reflect, as almost immediately she is presented the 'sad spectacle' (l. 57) of, as she supposes, Antonio and their children, dead. The stage direction following l. 55 makes it clear that these are '*artificial figures*', '*appearing as if they were dead*', but neither the Duchess nor the audience can know that they are not real. They are '*discovered*' (i.e., revealed) by a traverse curtain being drawn open, possibly by Bosola. What they look like can vary enormously; in the early productions they may well have looked quite serene in death, as did wax figures on the hearses or monuments of notables. In some modern productions they have been brought in on hospital trollies, or have looked like carcasses hanging from butchers' hooks; sometimes Antonio is without his left hand. Whatever the design, the spectacle is sufficiently forceful to convince the Duchess that he and the children are dead.

The crucial dynamic that now develops is based on the Duchess's 'Despair' (l. 74, 116), and her desire to die. How the rest of the play develops depends in part on how much the actor of the Duchess regards this despair as not simply psychological but spiritual. Theologically, despair is a loss of hope in salvation, and thereby closely related to pride, the worst of all sins. What develops in this French scene is a pattern of despairing intention by the Duchess followed by Bosola's offers of 'comfort' (l. 86; cf. the 'comfortable words' of the Anglican prayer book). Her first response to the dead bodies is to say that the sight 'wastes' her (l. 62), that it literally reduces her body. Then she says she would welcome death from being tied to 'that lifeless trunk' (l. 68; i.e., Antonio's corpse); this form of punishment was also used in emblem books as a symbol of ill-matched marriages. Her rejection of Bosola's 'Come, you must live' (l. 69) equates continued life with the torments of hell, so she threatens to commit suicide as Brutus's wife Portia did, by swallowing burning coals. Bosola responds to the threat of suicide with the reminder that despair (and hence suicide) are sins, and that she is 'a Christian' (l. 75). She retorts that since 'The church enjoins fasting' (l. 75) she can starve herself to death. By now her responses seem to have become quibbles for their own sake, from someone beyond interest in reasonable discourse. She has no interest if life; its brief and tedious nature is emphasized by a metatheatrical image of having been cast in a theatrical role against her will. Bosola's apparently sincere reaction is 'I pity you' (l. 88).

This scene between Bosola and the Duchess is briefly punctuated by a Servant she notices. Editors usually indicate that he enters here, though why he has entered is not made clear. He seems to exist only to allow the Duchess to use the line that a wish for long life is, to her, a curse. But he has also created a dynamic interruption in the scene, which now proceeds in a less frantic but more emotionally violent way. She abruptly changes her intention to pray to 'No, I'll go curse' (ll. 95–6), another un-Christian response. When she curses the stars, Bosola replies with the enigmatic 'the stars shine still' (l. 100), which has been taken as epitomizing the contradiction in Bosola's character. He may be utterly cynical, pointing out that the Duchess's curse has not worked (the sense to which she replies that it 'hath a great way to go', l. 101); or his line may be comforting, pointing to the stars in God's firmament. Her curse is now transferred to her brothers ('them', ll. 103 twice, 106, 108, 109; and 'they', 104). Her half-line at 108 offers her the opportunity to pause before the final climactic couplet, which is usually uttered in the throes of the most extreme despair. Presumably Cariola exits with her, and quite possibly the servants with torches, if only to allow Ferdinand and Bosola to be entirely alone for what follows.

111–142 'Excellent' (l. 111), declares Ferdinand as he enters. He has evidently been close by, listening, or possibly even observing. Referring to the 'presentations' as 'These' suggests that they are still on stage, and sometimes Ferdinand or Bosola will take some action with them to demonstrate the truth that they are merely 'framed in wax' (l. 112), not real bodies. This is normally, of course, a surprise to the audience, and invites a sudden realization that Ferdinand's purpose – 'To bring her to despair' (l. 117) – is to be achieved not merely with brutality, but with Ferdinand's idea of 'art' (l. 111). The demonic aspect of his character that has been hinted at before is now admitted: the Devil leads sinners to despair and damnation.

Most actors playing Bosola cannot help coming to admire (occasionally even love from afar) the Duchess by this point in the play. His response, 'Faith, end here' (l. 117), followed by urging Ferdinand to provide her with a 'penitential garment' (l. 119) and 'beads and prayer-books' (l. 121) suggests in addition a truly Christian response. That expression of Christian charity, whether real or assumed, certainly provides an effective foil for Ferdinand's 'Damn her!' (l. 121), with its literal meaning to the fore. He is still harping on her 'body' far more than her 'soul' (ll. 121–2). Bosola tries to refuse to see her again, before accepting with the proviso, 'Never in mine own shape' (l. 134), and the declaration that his 'business shall be comfort' (l. 137). His reference to 'this last cruel lie' may be accompanied by closing the curtain to hide the wax bodies. Ferdinand snorts sarcastically at Bosola's new-found conscience: 'Very likely!' As he continues with his own judgement that 'Thy pity is nothing of kin to thee' (l. 138), the audience may believe they by now know Bosola better than Ferdinand does.

Ferdinand ends the scene with hints about murdering Antonio, and a *sententia* about Ferdinand's intention to act the physician by giving the Duchess '*cruel*' (l. 142) medicine. Ferdinand may, by this stage in the play, foreshadow in intonation or movement his impending madness.

Act IV, scene ii

1 to the end   In this long and climactic scene the Duchess is tormented by madmen, prepared for death by Bosola in disguise, murdered under his supervision, along with Cariola and the two younger children, has her body gloated and agonized over by Ferdinand, then briefly revives before death, moving Bosola to profound pity and new determination. The action is macabre and grotesque, but also strangely ritualized. Looked at as a grotesque repetition and expansion of her marriage in Act I, incorporating elements of both epithalamiums (songs and poems in praise of bride and bridegroom) and court masques (and especially antimasques), one can see a masque structure determining the pattern of events. The masquers are announced, they enter and sing, then dance, before inviting the nobility in the audience to participate, and presenting the guest of honour with gifts before finishing with song and speeches. Viewed in this way, the scene progresses, as one reviewer put it, 'nicely poised between realism and ritual'.

1–37   The scene opens with the 'hideous' (l. 1) noise of the 'mad folk' (IV.i.128) Ferdinand threatened to torment her with, probably '*dismal*' (l. 60.2) discordant singing. This noise, or distortions of it, may continue off and on until the Madmen appear on stage. The Duchess (and Cariola) may be frightened by it as they enter, or the Duchess may display her ability to give 'a majesty to adversity' (IV.i.6), and sit down calmly herself before inviting Cariola to sit and tell her a tragic story to distract her. Her hair may be down for the first time in the play, a common signifier on the early modern stage for grief or distraction (or madness), and by l. 14 she has been weeping.

Cariola's attempts to comfort her mistress seem conventional and shallow compared to the depth of the Duchess's thought and emotion. She is in a state recognized by modern psychology, in which 'reason' (l. 6) in observation of a distorted external world may make her fear she is mad. She knows she is imprisoned, and that, to satisfy her brothers' anger over an action that was not a crime, she is unlikely to live much longer. Cariola comments on her musing (l. 16), which suggests the possibility of long silences during this French scene. Certainly in performance the Duchess has an opportunity to make a considerable emotional impact in the way she responds to her oppression, including paraphrasing classical Stoic authors on how to endure suffering (see ll. 27–30). Cariola is in many ways a foil to heighten the contrast. And if she did sit when the Duchess told her to earlier, she may jump up at the new 'noise' (l. 37), possibly from or related to the Madmen, that precedes the entry of the Servant.

37–44 A Servant enters, like the Announcer for a masque, to tell the Duchess of the 'sport' (l. 38) that she will be presented, for medicinal purposes to relieve her melancholy by inducing laughter. Although viewing lunatics was considered an entertainment in the seventeenth century, the audience already knows that Ferdinand's real purpose is to torment his sister, even to drive her mad herself. The small role of the Servant may be fundamentally a comic role (the description of the madmen is highly satiric, and he sounds as if he is himself amused), or he may be harsh to the Duchess, either deliberately (perhaps one of Ferdinand's henchmen) or simply because he is a brutal keeper and whipper-in of the Madmen (he may carry a whip to control them). The Duchess gives permission (at l. 44) that she, as a prisoner, is not in a position to withhold; but it is in character for her to do so both realistically, as her usual behaviour as a prince, and ritually, as the spectator of highest rank for the anticipated antimasque.

45–60 The Servant may describe the Madmen now, but delay their entry until after l. 60. Alternatively, following the cue of the Duchess's 'Let them come in' at l. 44), they may enter now so that each can be seen (and perhaps identified by occupational props or costume) one at a time. The first four mentioned may be the four main actors in the group, numbered 1 to 4 in the Q1 speech prefixes. A frequent theatrical assignment of roles identifies *First Madman* as the 'astrologian' (l. 47), *Second Madman* as the 'mad lawyer' (l. 45), *Third Madman* as the 'priest' (l. 45), and *Fourth Madman* as the jealous 'doctor' (l. 46), although not all their lines are clearly related to occupation. Q1 indicates that four of the principal actors probably doubled as Madmen, in addition to four hired men (see p. 7).

If the Madmen have come on at l. 45, there may be some business following the Duchess's 'Let them loose' (l. 59), perhaps involving untying or unchaining them, or more simply the Servant releasing them from his discipline. Production decisions here have included having the Madmen roped together in a long line, let out of a cage in which they have been wheeled in, and the Madmen starting a choreographed dance. Otherwise her line is the signal for them to enter.

60.1–114   One of the Madmen, who have either just been allowed in by the Servant or are now assembled by him (see note above), sings the song 'O, Let Us Howl' *'to a dismal kind of music'* (l. 60.2). Fortunately music for the song survives. It is attributed to Robert Johnson, a court musician who composed music for Shakespeare and other dramatists of the King's Men. A modern recording of 'O, Let Us Howl' (see p. 150) gives a sense of both how *'dismal'* it is intended to be, and how unusual in sudden musical shifts appropriate to a madman (a rising semitone on the word *'howl'*, for instance, that seems to make the word a howl). The words tend to reinforce the doom and disorder of the music. The personal pronouns in the song are plural (*'us'*, *'We'll'*, *'our choir'*, etc.), and in some productions all the Madmen have joined in the song. As a parody of an epithalamium (a marriage song) it could hardly be more grotesque and bestial (with the invitation to *'bill and bawl our parts'* (l. 66), and both music and words resolve into peaceful harmony only in contemplation of death (cf. 'swans'. l. 71).

In the early performances the Madmen would have been recognizably like performers of an antimasque, the grotesque prologue to the harmony and beauty of the main masque dances, poetry, song, and spectacle. The decorum of a masque is thoroughly breached both by the insanity of the characters, conveyed in striking images of disorder and terror ('my pillow is stuffed with a litter of porcupines', ll. 75–6), and by their sexual preoccupation ('Woe to the caroche that brought home my wife.…It had a large featherbed in it', ll. 104–6). Anti-Puritan jibes, and local jokes about the Blackfriars glassworks and constipated soap makers (an occupational hazard) are less easy for modern audiences to grasp. The mixture of satire and flashes of mordant wit in the midst of lunacy provides comedy and horror in a tricky balance.

How and whether this balance is constructively held depends in part on the reaction of the Duchess and Cariola. The Madmen, may, like Ferdinand, be a real threat, unpredictable and dangerous. Cariola is often so terrified that the Duchess has to comfort her as they are circled by the group, sometimes overtly threatened with rape or death. In the Royal Court production in 1971 the Madmen in fact advanced on the Duchess and killed her (thus shortening this scene considerably). But too much physical threat can miss the point that Ferdinand is applying psychological torture at this stage. Another production approach is to emphasize themes through grotesquery.

For instance, the actors of Ferdinand, the Cardinal, and other major roles may appear as Madmen metatheatrically representing perversions of themselves, displaying how the Duchess may see them now, or what she fears to become. A Madwoman may wear the Duchess's clothes, presenting her a distorting mirror of herself.

The '*dance*' with its '*music answerable thereunto*' (ll. 113.1–.2) may extend such display, and it provides an opportunity for directors, designers, and choreographers to emphasize further their own view of the play. In the seventeenth and eighteenth centuries the Madmen would have been foolishly laughable, but in the early twentieth century the dance became more abstract and expressionist, and since mid century ever more psychologically alarming and threatening, often now with elements of social, political, or religious critique. In a traditional marriage masque the dance would be, in keeping with the good wishes for future happiness, harmonious and beautiful; this parody of it for the Duchess is, whatever theatrical style is used, grotesque and ugly.

Bosola's entry after the dance seems the obvious place for the Madmen to leave. They may leave immediately following the dance, thus drawing attention to the lone figure of Bosola. He can revealed in their midst as a shock effect, and sometimes the Madmen are clearly frightened of him. Since the Servant says at l. 114 that he is leaving, he may again act as whipper-in, and herd the Madmen off the stage at that point.

115–64   Bosola is disguised '*like an old man*' (l. 113.2) in order to fulfil his masque role: in the original productions this almost certainly included long robes and a white beard, and possibly a hood to obscure his face. The audience will recognize him, but by theatrical convention the Duchess and Cariola fail to see through the disguise. Dressed as he is within the ritual of masque and epithalamium, he may appear to be an emblematic figure such as Time, Good Counsel, or Death. The protocol of the masque requires that after the dance the masquers would invite members of the audience to dance with them. Here Bosola incorporates the Duchess into the structure of the presentation.

Why does the Duchess not 'question him' (l. 114)? Possibly during a pause in which he may wait for her to do so she changes gear mentally. Perhaps she has started to understand the elaborate ritual in which she is being made a participant, or knows the figure in front of her is familiar ('dost know me?', l. 120), or simply accepts that the endgame is approaching. Or maybe Bosola sets the tone and agenda immediately in order to stamp his authority on what happens next. Either way, the statement that he has 'come to make [her] tomb' (l. 115) is realistically startling but ritually clear. Her implied denial of being near death (ll. 116–17) is answered by Bosola's 'worm-seed' speech (ll. 123–32). In the Christian *contemptus mundi* tradition, he asserts that things of this world are 'contemptible' (ll. 126–7), and his image of the 'soul in the body' being like 'a lark in a cage' makes explicit the contrast between this life and the afterlife in 'th'other world' (l. 19).

Nor does the Duchess's rank avail her anything; according to Bosola, as a 'great woman' she is even worse off than a 'milkmaid' (ll. 134, 136). Her grey hairs (cf. III.ii.58–60) indicate both aging and, now, death. The Duchess's famous assertion 'I am Duchess of Malfi still' (l. 141) may be delivered in a variety of ways. Sometimes it is a courageous assertion of her own integrity, sorrowful or defiant, sometimes a less amiable assertion of class superiority, occasionally almost a question. It fails to respond to Bosola's insistence that worldly position is nothing in the face of death. But his sententious couplet at ll. 143–4 is devastatingly clear about the hollowness of worldly fame and position ('*Glories*', l. 143). She seems to evade the seriousness of this '*old man*' in joking about fashion in tomb-making, but his reply about 'Princes' images' is both topical and deeply religious. She seems to respond with a change of tone and attitude, asking to 'know fully' (l. 162) the purpose of his 'preparation'. This is probably the moment when the Executioners enter.

165–94 The Executioners (at least three or four) carry a coffin, and what turn out to be strangling cords, and a handbell. The coffin carries an immediately clear implication of death, but Bosola continues his masque ritual by referring to it as 'a present' from Ferdinand and the Cardinal; the traditional gift from the masquers to the bride has here become death. Her request to 'see it' (l. 167) suggests that the coffin is covered with a cloth pall. When it is removed Bosola calls it her 'last presence chamber' (l. 170), recalling her formal throne chamber, the 'presence', in Act I, and stage arrangement can be designed to recall the earlier scene. Cariola's self-control breaks, and the contrast with the Duchess's calm is striking. Since the Duchess evidently accepts the gift of death, Bosola now announces himself as a new character, the 'common bellman' who visits condemned prisoners (see p. 92), and probably points the line by taking the bell from one of the Executioners. He will, he says, bring her to 'mortification' (l. 176); there is an important pun here, for he could mean to bring her to 'a state of torpor preceding death', or, simply, to 'death'; or, given the Christian underpinning of much of what he has said, to 'the subjection of appetites and passions' so that she will die in a state of grace, looking to salvation.

The dirge that now follows may well be chanted (fulfilling the structural position of the final song in the parodic wedding masque), and punctuated by ringing of the handbell as if Bosola were the 'common bellman' (l. 172). Its wedding imagery is inverted, with birds of ill omen, preparations for a grave ('Your length in clay', l. 182), and life and death described as a 'mist of error' and a 'storm of terror' respectively (ll. 87, 88). Ironically, the final preparations for death include some that match those of a bride: unbound hair strewn 'with powders sweet' (l. 189); the Duchess's hair, if unbound from the start of this scene may now be seen as ironically appropriate for a bride. She may have a '*crucifix*' (l. 192) about her neck, and given Ferdinand's diabolic associations, there is a sense in which Bosola's dirge is both preparing her for death and prescribing how she can avoid '*the foul fiend*' (l. 191). Now at midnight she is exhorted to '*come away*' (l. 194), a traditional joyful urging of the bride towards bed to consummate her marriage, but here to meet her bridegroom, Death.

195–204 Cariola's sudden, noisy, and probably violent attack on the Executioners and Bosola again underlines by contrast the Duchess's self-control. Reminders about the children's medicine and prayers introduce a note of pathos, as well as being designed to calm Cariola as she is dragged out by one or two of the Executioners, while at least two remain.

205–38 What follows is an astonishing moment in the theatre. 'What death?' 'Strangling: here are your executioners.' 'I forgive them' (ll. 205–6). Traditionally executioners kneel to ask forgiveness, and the Duchess calmly complies. She then develops her thought from mundane causes of death ('apoplexy, catarrh', l. 207) to strik-ingly metaphysical images ('throat cut / With diamonds...shot to death with pearls', 215–17), until she reaches the intensely baroque and modern concept of doors to death that may be opened from either side: by suicide or Death; or by murder or natural causes. At this point her calm shatters for a moment as the whispering of the Executioners (or in some productions, madmen or electronic susurration backstage) distracts her, but a moment later she is back in control with a standard misogynistic joke to them about women talking too much.

The moments leading up to her death are open to a variety of acting and staging possibilities. Perhaps she assists the executioners to place the cord about her neck, or holds her hair away from the nape of her neck, stressing her vulnerability. Or she may be dazed, and hardly aware what they are doing. Or perhaps she will still insist on her aristocratic rank. The reaction of Bosola may also draw atten-tion, for by now his admiration for her is clear. She takes control, ironically, by insisting on kneeling. (It is not clear when she stood up after the Madmen left, but presumably well before this point.) She kneels primarily to humble herself to enter 'heaven-gates' (l. 231), but the visual contrast with Bosola and the Executioners still standing is an implicit comment on them too. Her final message to her brothers, that they may 'feed in quiet' (l. 236), is a commonplace about relieving anxiety, but the audience may catch the irony of references earlier in the play to her brothers as wolves and other predators. Sometimes Ferdinand is above, watching; at Greenwich (1995) Simon Russell Beale grasped his own neck with his hand in twinship with his sister's strangulation.

The moment of death, strangled by a cord pulled usually by an Executioner on either side, has had too main possibilities for staging: first, an image of transcendence, reinforced by her kneeling, a crucifix at her breast, palms held out like icons of early martyrs, and a serene expression even as she dies; alternatively, an image that points to a meaningless death, the Duchess caught by surprise, or dying gruesomely with eyes bulging or neck snapping. In the first pity predominates for the audience, in the second horror, or intellectual critique. It may be terrifyingly real, or stylized or ritualistic. Bosola breaks the mood with abruptly efficient orders for killing Cariola and the children.

239–55   Cariola's death is utterly unlike that of the Duchess. Cariola demands justice, says she is betrothed, claims knowledge of treason, says she has not been confessed, and finally claims pregnancy in a desperate effort to avoid the fate of her mistress. The Executioners complain that she 'bites, and scratches' (l. 251), but eventually she is strangled in the same way as the Duchess ('wedding ring', l. 248, implies the loop of rope to go about her neck). Bosola deliberately tells the Executioners to leave the body of the Duchess on stage while they drag Cariola's off.

255–334   Ferdinand's re-entry, like that after the waxworks sequence in IV.i, suggests in realist terms that he may have been listening from a place of concealment. In more presentational terms, he enters because the play needs his reaction now. His first question, 'Is she dead?', confirms his preoccupation. He dismisses the dead children (probably revealed behind the arras, in a grotesque repeat of the waxworks scene), and fixes his eyes on the Duchess. Bosola pities the innocent children and the murdered Duchess; Ferdinand replies with three memorable and enigmatic sentences in one line: 'Cover her face; mine eyes dazzle; she died young' (l. 263). Detailed examination reveals parallels and sources such as dazzled eyes, blinded by light or misted with tears, being associated with spiritual blindness, and the proverb 'the good die young', but the effect in the theatre is likely to be of Ferdinand moved beyond words to see his sister dead (and perhaps at having been the cause). He reveals for the first time that they are twins, which may intensify the incest theme already observed in his character, especially in productions in which physical resemblance between the two of them is stressed.

Telling Bosola to 'Let me see her face again' (l. 271) suggests the two men may be crouched either side of her body, almost like 'wolves' (l. 258), on whom Ferdinand's mind is increasingly running, snarling over a corpse. His attack on Bosola for not interposing himself between 'her innocence and my revenge' (l. 277) is utterly ungrateful, but for the first time admits his own culpability. His explanation about wanting to inherit from her is entirely implausible, but his broken words about her marriage reinforce previous evidence of his obsession. The metatheatricality of describing Bosola as a 'good actor…playing a villain's part' (ll. 288–9; and see pp. 13–14) again reminds the audience that what they are seeing is a construct, not unmediated reality. We are urged to think about the meaning of the action.

Bosola is provoked by Ferdinand's hypocritical (or lunatic) shifting of the blame onto him, and responds by demanding the 'reward due to my service' (l. 293). Furthermore, Ferdinand now denies the responsibility he admitted a few moments earlier. Whether his outrageous mock-legal reasoning about how he had no 'authority' (l. 297) to have the Duchess executed is arrogant bluster or a mind operating under stress (or insanity) is for the actor to decide. So too is a decision about whether Ferdinand will pace the stage as he did in II.v, and whether he will make incipient madness evident to the audience. Bosola's invective about the brothers' hearts being 'Rotten, and rotting others' (l. 319) seems apt, and is followed in the same speech by an important moment as he says he is awaking from a dream. For the actor, the sincerity of this speech, and the direction(s) it takes him, are critical for the rest of the play. How much is he angry that he has been 'neglected' (l. 327), how much has he 'loathed the evil' (l. 330) he has done for Ferdinand, and what single or multiple motives will he now have? Ferdinand exits, in a way that may be clearly manic, to 'hunt the badger by owl-light' (l. 333).

335 to the end   Left alone with the body of the Duchess, Bosola repents his actions and loss of 'peace of conscience' (l. 339). Since he is alone with the audience, stage convention dictates that he probably means what he says. Often the actor will point the line 'Off, my painted honour!' (l. 335) by removing a disguise mask or cloak (see note to ll. 115–64). But his disguise has not in any sense been an 'honour'; this action will trivialize and obscure the real sense that he is renouncing the duplicity that has acquired him advancement in the world.

When he realizes the Duchess is still alive, his response is as extreme as a metaphysical love poem, urging her to assist him 'Out of this sensible hell' (l. 342), and promising to melt his frozen heart so that his blood will restore colour to her lips. He may cradle her in his arms. Her first word is 'Antonio' (l. 349), and Bosola's response is to tell her everything she would want to hear: that her husband is alive, her children alive, and her brothers reconciled to Antonio. Only the first is true, of course, but the Duchess utters the single word 'Mercy!' and dies, perhaps in peace, thinking it all to be true.

With the Duchess now truly dead, Bosola's 'guilty conscience' (l. 355) reveals itself to be 'a perspective' (l. 357), a Renaissance anamorphic or other distorted picture that appears to show one subject but, viewed from a particular angle, shows a quite different reality (in this case 'hell', l. 356). He recognizes his tears as 'penitent' (l. 364). Under the influence of his penitence, he picks up the Duchess (sometimes very tenderly, as if she were a sleeping child), and swears to deliver the body to the care of 'some good women' (l. 371), probably nuns. Then, he adds as a parting line, 'Somewhat I will speedily enact' (l. 373). What this will be remains unspecified, but he ends Act IV leaving us with an expectation of action (probably revenge) to follow in Milan in the final act.

Act V

Act V, scene i

1–17   Antonio's appearance – probably in disguise (see l. 69), and booted and spurred as recently arrived – establish that Antonio is now in Milan; a gesture from Delio at 'to Milan' (l. 4) will help make this clear. This is the third time the action following an act break has started with Antonio and his loyal friend re-establishing the scene and context. Delio is as suspicious of the two brothers as the Duchess was at the end of Act III, and he refers to even the honourable Marquis of Pescara having been forced to deprive Antonio of his lands on the basis of a legal fiction. When Pescara appears, Delio urges Antonio to hide himself while he will test what is happening to Antonio's land.

18–25   Delio's request for the lands that have reverted to Pescara is quickly refused. There is opportunity in performance, less easy to be sure of in reading, for the white-bearded Pescara to reinforce a sense of his 'noble nature' (l. 7), by gravity of deportment and of speech, evident sympathy for Antonio, or careful consideration before his friendly but elliptical indication that the request is 'Not fit for me to give nor you to take' (l. 23). He postpones further explanation, perhaps because he sees Julia entering.

25–36   The entry of Julia, 'the Cardinal's mistress' (l. 25) is likely to provoke close observation by Delio, given his parting from her in II.iv, and may well draw some reaction from her as well. Delio may remain at Pescara's side (since it is clear from ll. 37–8 that he hears Pescara give Antonio's lands to Julia), or he may move aside, though not out of earshot. Julia gives Pescara a letter in which the Cardinal asks for the lands for her, and Pescara's reply that he is glad to 'pleasure' (l. 33) her with the gift probably includes a sardonic reference to the sexual sense of the word. Her courtly thanks, however, offer no clue as to whether she has reacted to this, although we may see her do so, possibly with overtly sexual flirtation.

36–60   Delio's challenge to Pescara for refusing him but granting the suit to 'such a creature' (l. 40) is forcefully rejected. Pescara holds that it would compound immorality to give a gift acquired by 'injustice' (l. 46) to friends. Only 'a foul use' (l. 51) is appropriate for such a gift, in this case to the courtesan Julia, as 'salary for his lust' (l. 52; a gesture to the letter in his hand, or in the direction of the departed Julia, will make clear that 'his' refers to the Cardinal). Antonio's aside that Pescara 'would fright impudence / From sauciest beggars' (ll. 55–6) has sometimes been played as sarcastic. If played this way, Pescara's structural position in this final act of the play as a senior figure of integrity will be severely undermined (an option embraced by productions wishing to counter traditional 'tragic affirmation' at the end). But actors should note the morality of Webster's source (see pp. 95–104), Antonio's ''Tis a noble old fellow' at l. 60, the evident seriousness of Pescara's speech, and the respect Pescara is increasingly accorded as the play goes on, all coinciding to suggest that Antonio speaks with admiration. His final speech now, revealing Ferdinand's arrival in Milan, perhaps suffering from 'a frenzy' (l. 59), allows the audience to anticipate a crisis approaching.

60–77   As the scene returns to just Antonio and Delio a more sombre mood pertains (maybe supported by a change in lighting). Antonio's announcement that he has got 'private access' to the Cardinal's 'chamber' will reinforce the parallel to Ferdinand's visit to 'our noble Duchess' (ll. 65, 67), especially if he reveals a key such as that Bosola obtained for Ferdinand. While we are unlikely to share Antonio's naive hope of 'reconcilement' (l. 72), the fatalism of his final sententious couplet may raise him in our estimation. That he will go 'in mine own shape' (l. 69) is both brave, and possibly an indication that in this scene he has been disguised (possibly with a Pilgrim's robe from III.iv). If he and Delio exit together their enduring friendship will be reinforced.

Act V, scene ii

1 to the end   *This long and complicated scene, with entrances and exits creating many French scenes, has four main movements: first, presentation of the madness of Ferdinand; second, the Cardinal's pretended ignorance of the Duchess's death, and engagement of Bosola to kill Antonio; third, Julia's seduction and concealment of Bosola, and persuasion of the Cardinal to reveal his management of the murder of the Duchess and her children, and her resultant murder by the Cardinal; and finally Bosola's acceptance of the Cardinal's promise of reward for killing Antonio, and revelation that he intends instead to save Antonio and revenge the Duchess.*

1–26   Pescara's entrance with (or meeting) the Doctor may be signalled as the Cardinal's lodgings by having the Cardinal's Servant enter with the Doctor. The Doctor's appearance may well suggest a comic character (see reference to his beard and eyebrows at ll. 59–60), but initially he responds soberly to Pescara's questions: 'what's his disease?' and what is 'lycanthropia'? (ll. 4, 6). The description the Doctor gives of 'wolf-madness' matches that written by contemporaries of Webster (see pp. 94–5), who regarded it as an extreme form of jealousy. If so, Ferdinand's wish to dig up dead bodies may be read as a subconscious desire to reveal the murder of the Duchess (cf. IV.ii.308–10), and the experience of his skin being 'hairy … on the inside' (ll. 17–18) as the discomfort of the hair shirt of a penitent. The report of Ferdinand late at night howling like a wolf, and with 'the leg of a man / Upon his shoulder' (ll. 14–15), is a striking image of bestial savagery and madness. The horror approaches comedy as the Doctor boasts of how he will cure Ferdinand by beating him up if necessary, although the commonly prescribed cure of whipping for lunacy would have rendered the idea less extreme to Webster's audience.

27–83   The 1850 production had the lycanthropic Ferdinand enter 'with a slow prowling walk; dark haggard eyes; and disordered apparel', and others have given him a fur collar or lining for his costume, or a straitjacket, either worn or carried by an attendant. His acting, too, needs to reflect the madness. The grouped entry direction at the start of the scene in Q1 (see pp. 9–10) means that there can be no certainty that the Cardinal and Bosola enter at this point, but it seems most likely. Productions differ in whether to return the Cardinal to his robes now and for the rest of the play, or to keep him in the secular aristocratic (or sometimes modern military) clothing he adopts in III.iv for accepting a military commission; the first choice emphasizes further the hypocrisy and evil of this churchman, whereas the second is likely to draw more attention to the society within which the Duchess has been so powerfully suppressed. Bosola, probably in boots, spurs, and riding cloak (see l. 104), remains apart and watchful (apparently unseen by the Cardinal until l. 101). Grisolan and Roderigo might appear as additional courtiers.

Malateste's foolishness seems to provoke Ferdinand, and his leap (sometimes wolf-like) on to his shadow on the ground may be chilling as well as grotesque, or sometimes funny. Guilty fear of one's shadow is found in Renaissance proverbs and emblem books. Pescara evidently steps forward to replace Malateste at Ferdinand's side, urging him to stand up, but not provoking him; and Ferdinand's position on the stage floor perhaps suggests the image of following at eye-level a team of snails.

The Cardinal (who might only arrive on stage at this moment) insists on Ferdinand being raised to his feet and held. At this point the Doctor steps in, possibly shouting at Ferdinand, or otherwise irritating him. Ferdinand's demand that the Doctor's beard and eyebrows be reduced might indicate an elderly dignified figure; but his prose speech, his bizarre language and actions, the removal of his gown at l. 70, and his humiliation by Ferdinand before his exit all suggest that the beard and shaggy eyebrows may be comedy makeup. In the earliest productions it is possible the boy playing Cariola also played the Doctor (but see p. 7); if so, such makeup would do much to disguise the fact. The Doctor now hectors Ferdinand with potential remedies, some of them symbolically linked to his past actions and experience (e.g., treatment for 'cruel sore eyes', ll. 64–5, may recall 'mine eyes dazzle', IV.ii.263, and his insistence on visiting the Duchess in darkness). In his madness Ferdinand is afraid of the aggressive Doctor, whom we see breaching court decorum by removing his gown. (By the early eighteenth century stage tradition had developed so far towards comedy that he took off four gowns, one after the other, just as the Gravedigger in *Hamlet* at the time removed multiple waistcoats.) An attempt by Ferdinand to free himself probably initiates the Doctor's taunt 'Can you fetch a frisk, sir?' (i.e., cut a caper; l. 73), and in some productions the Doctor has responded with his own little dance, enraging Ferdinand. The Q4 stage direction '*Throws the Doctor down and beats him*' at 'Hence, hence!' (l. 79) is a natural development from Ferdinand's threats, and physical violence may have started earlier. Ferdinand has clearly broken free, is probably chasing courtiers as well, and is able to exit unimpeded. No exit is specified for the Doctor, but a quick departure here can add to the comedy; and the Doctor's line can be played as aside to the audience. This whole section of Ferdinand's madness invites a great variety of performance, from slapstick comedy to outright horror.

84–103   Horror appears to be Bosola's reaction to the 'fatal judgement' (l. 84) fallen on Ferdinand. This may result from him observing all the action; or his entry may be delayed until just before Ferdinand's exit, setting up a parallelism with the Cardinal if he also had a late entry at l. 52 (see note above). The Cardinal has every reason to be 'wondrous melancholy' (l. 201), and it should probably appear now in the acting, as it does in his aside. He is concerned to distract attention from anything suspicious that Ferdinand may reveal in his madness, so concocts a mysterious ghost story to explain to Pescara and others how his brother fell mad. They are polite enough to accept the story, and to recognize the Cardinal's evident desire to be left alone with Bosola.

104–19   Once alone with Bosola the Cardinal, surprisingly, confirms to the audience that he must conceal his involvement in the Duchess's murder. He therefore asks after her health, and also promises Bosola advancement even if Ferdinand should die. Bosola evidently looks 'wildly' when the Cardinal seems ignorant of her death, and accepts with alacrity the offer of doing 'one thing' for the Cardinal; action will be a relief from 'musing much' (ll. 111, 114, 119).

120–21   This tiny French scene serves as a brief structural transition from Bosola's apparent disorientation at the Cardinal seeming not to know of the death of the Duchess, to what seems a calmer assessment in what follows. The entry of Julia, and her very obvious (and comic) relation to the audience of her attraction to Bosola (contrasting sharply with the Cardinal's brusque dismissal of her), is only a brief interruption to the continuing suspicious assessment of each other by the Cardinal and Bosola.

122–44 When the Cardinal demands that Bosola find and kill Antonio (so that the Duchess can remarry!), Bosola's response seems mainly designed to draw the Cardinal out. When he says how much he desires to see 'that wretched thing, Antonio', the audience will understand it as the exact opposite of the Cardinal's belief that Bosola is agreeing to kill Antonio.

145–50 Left alone on stage, Bosola can reveal to the audience what he has been concluding since the Cardinal started talking too him. The audience will no doubt agree that the Cardinal does 'breed basilisks in 's eyes' (l. 145), the basilisk or cockatrice being a fabled creature so dangerous that its breath, or even seeing it, was fatal. Bosola is sufficiently suspicious to tell us that he will be as crafty as the old fox the Cardinal.

150–222 Julia's sudden re-entry armed with a pistol straight after the Cardinal's exit is a striking replay of Antonio's re-entry in III.ii after Ferdinand's exit, just as the wooing of a man by a woman that now follows is a parodic repeat of the Duchess and Antonio in I.i (see p. 138). And there is comedy in the fact that both characters are well aware of the inversion of the norm. Bosola's first reaction is alarm and an attempt to escape, but Julia has locked the doors. The accusation of 'treachery' (l. 152) at pistol-point will convince Bosola of the seriousness of the threat, but Julia's explanation that she is accusing Bosola of putting 'Love-powder' (l. 155; and see III.i.63–77) in her drink will raise a huge laugh from the audience, especially if Bosola is slower to comprehend her meaning. By ll. 164–5, however, he has disarmed and armed her (i.e., embraced her within his arms), nearly always with her enthusiastic co-operation ('you'll say / I am wanton', ll. 168–9). He is initially suspicious, but becomes convinced of her infatuation and resolves to 'work upon this creature' (l. 183). Just as

Delio tried to do in II.iv, he will try to obtain information from Julia about the Cardinal.

Bosola now pretends to succumb to Julia's charms, and becomes 'amorously familiar' (l. 184), which in some productions becomes very familiar indeed. Julia's description of herself as one of the 'great women of pleasure' (l. 192) confirms her status as a courtesan, but perhaps more importantly increases the grotesque parody of the Duchess and Antonio's wooing scene in Act I. Her offer to do something for Bosola plays into his hands, and he instantly demands that she ascertain why the Cardinal has become 'wondrous melancholy' (l. 201). She is so keen to gratify her lust by proving her devotion to Bosola that she instantly installs him in hiding where he will be able to hear and possibly even 'see' (l. 221) her extract the information from the Cardinal. It is possible she hears his approach, which puts pressure on them both ('Go, get you in'; l. 220), and drives the action forward.

In this entire section much of the tone, and the extent to which parallelism and parody of I.i and III.ii are stressed, will depend on both acting and costume, especially of Julia. She is often played as coarse and blatantly sexual from her first entry, but it is possible to play within a decorum that relies largely on words. Some modern productions have portrayed her as a victim of sadism, or even as a masochist desiring such treatment. Much will depend on how she carried herself in I.i and V.i, and especially II.iv. Also, the way in which various productions use comedy in Act V is important, since comedy seems to increase in this act in tandem with horror and tragedy. Some productions try to alternate strong comedy with fierce horror so as to use the comedy to exhaust or defuse in advance any audience tendency to laugh when suffering becomes extreme. Not comic relief, but comic pre-emption.

223–79 As the Cardinal enters he calls or speaks to one or more Servants, insisting that no-one should have access to Ferdinand without his knowledge. The Servants probably exit, and the Cardinal again shares with the audience his anxiety that Ferdinand in his madness 'may reveal the murder' (l. 226). He may be carrying a book (in the Renaissance a common emblem of melancholy, as in *Hamlet* II.ii and III.i); or the book that will be needed later in the scene may be in a pocket, or hidden (or displayed) onstage. It may be a bible (since Julia swears upon it 'most religiously', l. 275). He also indicates that he is deeply weary of Julia, whom he brutally calls his 'ling'ring consumption' (a line that often raises a laugh; l. 227).

Julia's approach to him is, ironically, and as the audience now knows, the worst possible time she could have chosen to try to elicit the cause that makes him 'sad' (l. 236). How much the actor of Julia uses her sexual wiles in addition to clever argument varies greatly in production. The Cardinal tries to fob her off with the proverbial misogynist jibe that the only way for a woman to keep a secret is not to be told it, but parsimony in sharing information is also standard in the gathering of intelligence: now called 'need to know'.

The Cardinal first retreats to a hypothetical admission ('imagine I have committed / Some secret deed', l. 250–51), and, ironically, explains the danger to her if she were to 'receive a prince's secrets' (l. 259). The danger of 'prince's secrets' is at the heart of the tragedy of the Duchess, and the Cardinal's warning to Julia is more honest than perhaps either of them can conceive.

Finally (perhaps in evident weariness, irritation, anger, or sadness) the Cardinal tells Julia (and the audience learns fully for the first time) that he directed the death of the Duchess and her two younger children. Her immediate exclamation of horror at what he has done evidently makes him think that she is so shocked that she will be unable to keep his secret, and he will understand 'It lies not in me to conceal it' (l. 273) in this sense. The audience, of course, knows that she speaks literally: because the hidden Bosola has also heard the Cardinal's revelation, the secret is not hers alone. She may glance towards the door or arras where Bosola is hidden to remind the audience of his proximity. The Cardinal has ready access to a book (see above), but whether he now smears poison on it, or always has a poisoned book (and not just the poison) ready to hand, is an interesting question, especially if it is a bible (which would increase the anti-Catholic element of the play; see p. 3). The former choice means the audience is aware of the cold-blooded murder as it unfolds; the latter means that only at l. 277 ('thou'rt poisoned with that book') will they realize that the apparent oath is yet another devilish manipulation of religion by the Cardinal. Similarly, the Cardinal may apply brutal pressure to force Julia's lips hard into the book, or may allow Julia to give a true (but equivocal) oath with her 'Kiss' (l. 275) that she will not herself reveal the secret. The effect is slightly different with the two stagings (especially if offstage madmen's cries or abstract sound effects accompany the murder), but either way the Cardinal explains his decision with Machiavellian detachment. It is this explanation that brings Bosola bursting onto the stage.

280–87 There is no need for Bosola to have drawn his sword or dagger, or be carrying Julia's pistol, but the possibilities are there. More important is the manner of Julia's death: forgiving her executioner, and accepting the appropriateness of his 'justice' (l. 281), since she had, indirectly, revealed the Cardinal's secret. Bosola's sardonic question ('Couldst not thou have poisoned him?', l. 286) is typical of the juxtaposition of black comedy with deep tragedy that increases in Act V. Her response is that of the villain/heroine of Webster's earlier tragedy *The White Devil*: that she dies going 'I know not whither' (l. 288). This was a traditional phrase for a dying sinner, although some critics (and productions) have interpreted it as an existentialist or ungodly questioning of the Christian concept of salvation. She usually dies cradled by Bosola, the second time in the play he has done this, and a further reminder of the strange parallels between Julia and the Duchess.

287–328 Julia's death brings Bosola and the Cardinal into the confrontation towards which this scene has been building. As in IV.ii, Bosola and one of the Duchess's brothers argue over the corpse of a woman just murdered, and Bosola seeks reward for his services (though how much the initial demand is serious, and how much an outburst of frustration and anger, is for the actor to determine). The Cardinal's first response is to threaten Bosola, but Bosola scorns the threat. He remains deeply suspicious of the Cardinal, and his caustic comments about the likelihood that the Cardinal might try to kill him (ll. 296–300) is truth spoken in malcontent jest. Nevertheless, he seems to accept the Cardinal's offer of 'honours' (l. 303), and confirms his previous agreement to kill Antonio. The Cardinal is evidently thinking on his feet, and gives Bosola the 'master key / Of our lodgings' (ll. 326–7) so that he can remove Julia's body secretly. A duplicate key was crucial in Act III, and the audience has more recently heard in V.i that Antonio also has a key to the Cardinal's lodging. The Cardinal stresses how the key is a measure of the 'trust' (l. 328) he is placing in Bosola, and an important element in performance is whether either character displays his real lack of trust to the audience. If the Cardinal arrogantly leaves the moment he stops speaking, the double meaning of Bosola's half line reply, 'You shall find me ready' (l. 328), is more pointed.

329 to the end   Bosola is again alone with the audience, and able to think through the implications of Ferdinand's madness, the Cardinal's promise of reward, the truth about the Cardinal's initiating the murder of the Duchess (which has led to the death of Julia), and the danger ('slippery ice-pavements', l. 332) that his own 'pity' (l. 330) is leading him into through his promise to find and kill Antonio. The 'precedent' (l. 334) of what happens to anyone who crosses the Cardinal is lying on the stage before him in the form of Julia. 'Security' (overconfidence) is 'the suburbs of hell' (l. 336); not merely dangerous in this world, but endangering salvation in the next. At the moment he asserts his continuing intention to defy the Cardinal, try to save Antonio, and perhaps achieve revenge for the Duchess, he sees her – 'There, there!' (l. 345). In Webster's *The White Devil* a stage direction specified the entry of a ghost in a similar situation, despite the character who sees the ghost dismissing it as an illusion conjured up by his 'melancholy' (l. 346). The ghost of the Duchess might appear on stage to Bosola at this point, in order to physicalize the sense of her influence in Act V. But the point is the same even if the audience does not see the ghost, and Bosola will '*start*' (Q4 stage direction) when he thinks he sees her. Her death has changed him, as his final couplet – welcoming penitence as the route to salvation – makes clear. His final exit with Julia's body may be acted to resemble the manner in which he took the Duchess's body off stage. The body in his arms will in any case give force to his hope that 'Penitence' will 'raise [him] up' (ll. 347–8).

Act V, scene iii

1–19   Although Delio's first sentence, 'Yon's the Cardinal's window' (l. 1) indicates he and Antonio have reached their destination as planned in V.i, and implies imminent action, in fact the scene is largely reflective. The two actors have to find the transition in mood, and part of that can be the physical sense of arrival. They probably carry torches or lanterns to indicate it is 'about the mid of night'

(V.i.66), and modern productions tend to use dim, shadowy, and very atmospheric lighting, since Delio says the Cardinal's defensive palace was built from the ruins of an abbey, and draws attention to part of a cloister wall famous for its 'dismal' (l. 6) echo. If '*the Duchess' grave*' was a large property at the Blackfriars and Globe (see p. 6), it was likely upstage with the tiring house wall representing the cloister), and therefore Antonio and Delio probably downstage at the greatest distance they can be, facing it. The locale induces in both men thoughts of mortality, even of 'doomsday' (l. 17), when all the dead (not just 'spirit[s]', l. 8), arise from their graves for the Day of Judgement. Antonio develops this into a meditation on the ephemeral and misleading nature of worldly 'security' (V.ii.336), on which wealthy men relied to lie safe after death in stone vaults, undisturbed until 'doomsday'.

20–42   The foreboding voice of the Echo, presumably played by the actor of the Duchess, and coming from her grave, transforms this scene from verbal meditation to active involvement of the spirit of the Duchess. Her tone is foreboding ('*A thing of sorrow*', l. 24), her meaning repeated warnings to Antonio ('*Do not*', '*Be mindful of thy safety*', '*fly your fate!*', ll. 29, 32, 35). In this she literally echoes Delio's urging that Antonio should abandon his rash plan to visit the Cardinal. Antonio argues with Delio, and eventually with the Echo itself at ll. 38–9, but evidently reacts strongly to the final echo, '*Never see her more*' (l. 42). As Antonio describes the moment in his following speech, it is a visual moment in which 'on the sudden' he sees a face, presumably that of the Duchess, 'folded in sorrow' (ll. 44–5). Like Bosola's experience in the previous scene, this may be simply Antonio's melancholy, 'your fancy, merely', as Delio puts it at l. 46, although even then the audience will no doubt see a physical reaction from Antonio. But there is evidence of the physical appearance of such a ghost from a tomb in another play in the King's Men's repertoire about this time (see p. 6), so it is entirely possible that the Duchess (probably the same boy actor in both plays) was meant to appear within a vault on stage, illuminated by a special light (real or imagined). Nineteenth-century productions had elaborate lighting effects of the Duchess slowly vanishing amongst trees at the back of the stage, described by critics as spectral. In modern productions she is sometimes on stage throughout much or all of Act V, observing or even supervising the action. This physicalization is a theatrical response to the strong textual emphasis on her continuing influence on Bosola, Antonio, and others in this act. However the scene is staged (and even if the Duchess is on stage, it is clear that Delio does not see her), it can hardly be regarded as realistic, and therefore its emblematic nature must be embraced theatrically for it to succeed.

43 to the end   Following his vision of the Duchess, Antonio finally moves into action, and Delio says he will fetch Antonio's elder son (the only child of his secret marriage still alive). Antonio's final speech of farewell seems to foreshadow death after 'noble suff'rings' (l. 57), paralleling the Duchess's resignation in Act IV. Since the two men are likely to exit in different directions, there may well be an embrace or other strongly-marked leave taking from these two close friends and allies as Antonio determines to risk everything.

Act V, scene iv

1–21   The sudden appearance of the Cardinal, surrounded by courtiers and no doubt servants with torches, immediately after the exit of Antonio with Delio, has a theatrical force of making their meeting seem imminent. The Cardinal's prohibition on the courtiers staying up to sit with Ferdinand is so strongly urged as to provoke some resistance from the aristocratic Pescara and the foolish Malateste. The Cardinal's elaborate demand that they swear to it is likely to strike the audience as strange, just as it does the courtiers. They all agree to swear to it as the Cardinal demands, however, though Pescara and Malateste indicate their irritation, Malateste so ineptly as usually to raise a laugh. In a brief transition while the Cardinal '*Withdraws*' (l. 18; i.e. walks apart but remains on stage), the courtiers, as they start to exit, comment on the 'foul storm' (l. 18), for which some productions have provided realistic or abstract sound effects; and more overtly than ever before on the association of Ferdinand with the Devil.

22–31   Briefly the Cardinal is alone with the audience, and his explanation for the previously mysterious injunction to keep the courtiers away from his lodgings in the palace (which is evidently where Ferdinand is housed as well) matches audience knowledge of the arrangements the Cardinal has made with Bosola to remove Julia's corpse. Mention of 'Julia's body' (l. 25) is followed instantly by an admission of conscience, and an inability to pray (i.e., the mortal sin of despair). For the Cardinal, so guarded and reticent through most of the play, to admit this to the audience suggests huge strain. Returning to plot matters, he says it is the time appointed for Bosola to arrive to get Julia's body, and that once that is done he will ensure Bosola's death. Virtually all the torches or candles on stage that indicate night will have left with the courtiers and attendants, or do so now as the Cardinal exits. The audience must imagine the stage in darkness.

32–3 Bosola enters and is alone on stage. Either he has heard the Cardinal threaten his 'death' (l. 33) while he was still offstage, or he may enter before the Cardinal leaves, and overhear his last few lines. Modern productions usually employ shadowy or blue lighting to reinforce the sense of darkness on which the action now depends. Bosola hears someone's 'footing' (l. 33), but cannot see who approaches.

34–8 Ferdinand's distracted and partly whispered speech about strangling, agreement, and insistence that 'it must by done i'th' dark' (l. 37) is heard by Bosola, standing apart listening in the (imagined) dark. But Bosola gives no indication of recognizing Ferdinand's voice, and may not know he has left.

39–50 Bosola continues the interrupted sharing of his thoughts with the audience, noting that serious crimes always require even more serious crimes. When Antonio and his Servant enter, the audience is reminded of the darkness by the Servant leaving to fetch a 'dark lantern' (l. 43). In some productions Antonio has knelt at the Cardinal's *prie dieu*, the action provoking his thought about taking the Cardinal 'at his prayers' (l. 44; cf. *Hamlet* III.iii.75). Bosola may take these words to refer to him, and again failing to recognize a voice, he quickly stabs Antonio, presumably thinking he is either the Cardinal or a hired assassin.

50–72 When the Servant returns with the lantern, he needs to search for his master. Presumably when he finds Antonio the lantern light allows Antonio to recognize 'Bosola!', and Bosola 'Antonio!' (ll. 51, 52). Q1 prints a query following both names; although queries often served as exclamation marks, both acting options are available: astonishment, or uncertainty. Bosola, who may be cradling this third victim in his arms too, is appalled at his 'misprision' (l. 80), his mistake in murdering the 'man I would have saved' (l. 53). 'We are the stars' tennis balls' (l. 54) he says bleakly, the victims of wanton gods. Antonio's response to learning that the Duchess and the two younger children are 'murdered' (l. 59) is not to look forward in any positive sense as the Duchess did, but only to welcome it as the end of 'vexation' (l. 69). His final exhortation, that his son should 'fly the courts of princes' (l. 72), matches Vittoria's dying lines in Webster's *The White Devil* in pointing to the consistent critique in both plays of the corrupt power of most 'princes'. Beyond this socio-political theme may lie another contrast, that between the Duchess transcending worldly concerns in order to face the implications of a Christian death, and Antonio still concerned with matters of this world even as he dies.

73 to the end   Bosola's apparent anger at the Servant explaining Antonio's mission of reconciliation to the Cardinal suggests strong passion within Bosola. He instructs the Servant to pick up Antonio's body, then turns to the audience to express his sense of urgency in finding the Cardinal to 'bring him to th' hammer' (l. 80). Bosola's sudden exclamation in the middle of the line, 'O direful misprision!' marks a change of thought so abrupt that it seems likely that his attention has been drawn to Antonio, perhaps by now on the Servant's back. His determination to be his 'own example' (l. 82) parallels Antonio welcoming the opportunity 'To appear myself' (l. 50).

Act V, scene v

1–7   Candles or torches may have been brought on to indicate that the scene is no longer in darkness; in modern productions the lighting will change, and design elements from previous scenes in the Cardinal's lodgings may reappear. Although the Cardinal entering '*with a book*' signals melancholy (see note to V.ii.223–79), and may recall the book that poisoned Julia, its specifically devotional character becomes clear from the Cardinal's comments to the audience. Questions about hell are uncomfortable for 'a guilty conscience', and panic is implicit in the Cardinal's terrifyingly ambiguous image of 'a thing, armed with a rake' that seems to 'strike' (ll. 4–7) at him, punctuated by Bosola's entry.

7–19   The Cardinal will not notice the Servant with Antonio's body until l. 37, as his attention seem entirely taken up with Bosola's 'ghastly' look, and the mixture of 'some great determination' and 'fear' in his face (ll. 8–10). This tableau is presumably resolved by Bosola drawing his sword on 'Thus' (l. 10) as much as by what he says. Bosola confidently dismisses any possibility of the guard hearing the Cardinal's cries for help, as he does the large bribe. He may emphasize that he has 'confined [the Cardinal's] flight' (l. 17) by locking doors. The Cardinal's fear and loud shouting will be the most striking features of this short section, although cowardice was often associated with the phlegmatic temperament.

19–33   In the Jacobean theatre Pescara, Malateste, and other courtiers entered at the upper level (note their refusal to go 'down' at ll. 22 and 31), possibly with lights of their own, and perhaps in night attire that will signal the late-night disruption caused by the Cardinal's cries. Their lines make it clear (as will, therefore, their acting) that the audience is to understand that they can hear the Cardinal, but not see him. Otherwise they would see that 'the sword's at my throat!' (l. 26). The irony of the Cardinal's insistence in V.ii that they not come to his lodgings is emphasized by mockery from the foolish Malateste and Roderigo. Pescara, however, the wisest among them, determines to 'force ope the doors' if necessary. In modern productions the difficulty of controlling the comedy, and sometimes the lack of an upper or separate stage area, often results in this French scene being cut entirely. Comedy and tragedy are clearly juxtaposed, though, and those productions that meet the challenge have to find a tone that allows them to interrelate; the audience *frisson* when this conjunction is achieved is often regarded as a particular hallmark of Websterian tragedy.

34–47   As the characters at the upper level exit, Bosola '*kills the Servant*' with professional efficiency so that he cannot 'let in rescue' (ll. 34–5). Bosola has some slight justification if the Servant has tried to 'unbarricade the door' (l. 35) first. The Cardinal evidently sees

Antonio's body for the first time as Bosola points to it ('Look there', l. 37). When Bosola instructs him to 'Pray' (l. 39) as a preparation for death, he may also prepare his sword with some formality to become the emblematic 'sword' of 'Justice' (ll. 41, 40). The Cardinal probably falls to his knees as he begs for 'mercy!' (l. 41), but Bosola stabs (or in some modern productions shoots) the Cardinal with no mercy. Only at this stage does the Cardinal fight back, determining not to die in a cowardly manner 'Without any resistance' (l. 46). He probably pulls Bosola down, given his later account of them 'struggling / Here i'th' rushes' (ll. 88–9), referring to the fresh rushes with which the floors of palaces and the stages of early modern theatres were alike strewn.

47–79 This short French scene is perhaps the most difficult to stage, given the grotesquery of Ferdinand's lycanthropia, mortal wounds to all three characters on stage, and their substantial speeches of summation and philosophy. Such dying speeches were a convention of Elizabethan and Jacobean theatre, but are harder for modern audiences to accept, especially in realist productions. Ferdinand charges on stage in his madness thinking he is in the midst of a desperate battle (for the metatheatrical joke about needing a horse, see p. 8). Ferdinand may act as a mad warrior, or possibly stress the lycanthropia (in the 1980 Manchester Royal Exchange production he entered howling out of the darkness, leaping at Bosola's throat like a werewolf). It seems he triumphantly waves his sword over Bosola and the Cardinal in their '*scuffle*' on the floor (l. 53 SD; see previous note), and stabs his brother when he believes him to be fighting for 'the adverse party' (l. 52).

Since the Cardinal at this point utters a sententious couplet, his death can be assumed to be close. Ferdinand, uninjured, and having given Bosola '*his death wound*' (l. 53 SD), now offers a bizarre contrast of classical precedent and toothache as he lectures both of them on lessons of bearing pain and death. Bosola, however, manages to give Ferdinand a mortal wound, and is elated at succeeding in his revenge before he dies. Ferdinand revives enough to reflect on his life: his repeated cry of 'My sister!' as 'the cause' (l. 71) raises the possibility that he is recognizing the long-suppressed reality of his destructive desire for her. Although the phrase '*cut with our own dust*' in his *sententia* suggests a kind of nemesis, a punishment to fit the crime, rhyming '*lust*' with '*our own dust*' (ll. 72–3) may be intended to suggest their shared '*dust*'. Ferdinand may die in the Cardinal's arms. In the nineteenth century it became common for a melodramatic vision to appear above of Antonio (another actor playing Antonio's body on stage) reunited with the Duchess in heaven as Ferdinand stretched out his arm towards her and died. This apotheosis of course replaces the play's complex focus on Bosola at this point with an easy sentimentality.

Bosola responds to the Cardinal's observation or jibe that Bosola too is dying (which must be evident in his acting), with satisfaction at his revenge, and an image of the Cardinal as 'a huge pyramid' mounting, as its design requires, to 'a little point, a kind of nothing' (ll. 77, 79).

80–108 Sometimes a sound of the doors being forced open is heard just before Pescara and the other courtiers burst in. The stage now has three dead bodies, and two more dying, a vision of 'sad disaster' (l. 80). While Pescara immediately tends to the Cardinal, Bosola explains his 'Revenge, for the Duchess of Malfi' (l. 81), perhaps gesturing at 'th' Aragonian brethren'; for Antonio, also visible on stage; for Julia, poisoned by 'this' Cardinal; and with surprising honesty, for himself, for not being rewarded ('Neglected') despite being the agent of all this against his own 'good nature' (ll. 81–7). The Cardinal comes to life just long enough to express concern for Ferdinand (seeming not to realize he is dead), and to desire only to be 'laid by, and never thought of' (l. 90).

Pescara recognizes the irony of the Cardinal's precautions to prevent him being disturbed, whereas Malateste in high indignation demands explanation of the blood-covered Bosola ('Thou…thing of blood', l. 92; cf. *Coriolanus*, II.ii.109). Bosola's reply repeats the 'Mist' (l. 94) that many of Webster's tragic characters face when they die, but then instantly switches to saying it was 'Such a mistake as I have often seen / In a play' (ll. 95–6), such an intensely metatheatrical image that the actor will need to decide how much laughter to allow, and whether it should be quickly suppressed. He goes on to profound seriousness, following the Renaissance stage convention that dying characters speak truth. Despite the 'pain', he has no regrets at dying as a result of his revenge 'in so good a quarrel' (l. 100). Acknowledging his experience of 'this gloomy world' as a 'deep pit of darkness' (ll. 100–101), he nevertheless continues, despite the contradictions inherent in his actions in the play, to his final couplet implying that his actions have, at the last, been 'just' (l. 104). He adds another line after this neat finish, however, a qualification or perhaps admission of his guilt as he dies: 'Mine is another voyage' (l. 105). The death of Bosola marks the resolution of the revenge plot following the death of the Duchess; and also the culmination of the violence and evil of the tragedy.

Pescara breaks the mood of exhaustion by announcing the imminent arrival of Delio with Antonio's elder 'son and heir' (l. 108).

109 to the end   Conventionally, Elizabethan and Jacobean tragedies end with a restoration of order, hierarchy, and to some extent virtue. Pescara, the courtier most identified as virtuous and reasonable, ushers in Delio and the 'young, hopeful gentleman' (l. 112) who is the eldest child of Antonio and the Duchess, and certainly Antonio's 'heir' (l. 108). To establish him 'In 's mother's right' (l. 112) is a more difficult question. If there really is already a young 'Duke of Malfi ... she had by her first husband' (III.iii.69–70), then her elder son by Antonio can only inherit his mother's private wealth, not the duchy. But most audiences will have forgotten about the other son (and indeed most productions cut the III.iii reference to him, assuming it is a loose end that Webster failed to tidy up). The moral force of presenting on stage the eldest child of the love between the Duchess and Antonio means that audiences and readers accept him as the heir to Malfi, to his 'mother's right', and to their love, virtue, and integrity. Delio's speech deplores the 'eminent things' (i.e., her brothers) who leave nothing behind them. All that lasts 'beyond death', as many poets have said, is a reputation for '*Integrity*' (l. 120). The well-known classical precept of *integer vitae*, integrity of life, means a Stoic honesty, or wholeness, in facing the evil and suffering of life; or, in its Christian application, the virtuous life and spiritual belief that will lead to salvation.

Stagings of this final scene may support a Renaissance convention of the re-establishment of rule, harmony, and virtue by having Pescara and others kneeling to the new Duke, or otherwise showing an unqualified commitment to the heir of the Duchess of Malfi. Some modern productions, however, have found that they cannot reconcile this resolution with the cynical pessimism they believe the play to represent. Sometimes, therefore, they cut this final French scene, ending instead with Bosola's dying lines. Others render it ambiguous in its staging, by, for instance, presenting a very young and nervous boy isolated by staging or light in the midst of threatening dangerous adults; or preventing the boy from pulling Antonio out of the pile of bodies; or even dressing him to look like a miniature Ferdinand, thus implying that the sinister cycle will start again. Productions that follow the sense of the final lines are more likely, as in 1960, to have him go and kneel or weep by Antonio, or as in 1980, to finish with bright light and pure, swelling music.

3   Sources and Cultural Context

John Webster (c. 1578–c. 1634–38), like William Shakespeare, grew up in the Elizabethan cultural climate, and experienced the political, religious, economic, and social uncertainty that accompanied the final years of Elizabeth's reign and transition to the rule of James VI (of Scotland) and I (of England). But Webster was a generation younger, and Shakespeare was retiring as the King's Men's principal dramatist by the time Webster was writing this play. And Webster, unlike Shakespeare, was London born and bred. His father ran the family firm, building and hiring out coaches, and was a 'Citizen' of the City of London by virtue of his membership of the Guild of Merchant Taylors, an honour the dramatist assumed after his father's death. Thus, Webster was a gentleman, and lived in the midst of the greatest metropolis of Europe in a position of some prosperity.

His education was most likely at the famous Merchant Taylors' School, where his humanist studies would have included Greek and especially Latin. He may have taken part in the plays that were encouraged as a way of enlarging the study of rhetoric. Following school he appears to have enrolled at the Inns of Court in London; while there is no evidence of his ever practising law, all his plays demonstrate his fascination with legal process. Mixing with gentlemen and graduates of the only two universities in England (Oxford and Cambridge) during his legal training at the Inns of Court would have brought Webster in touch with the nexus of law, money, birth, education, religion, political power, revenge, corruption, and occasional virtue that pervade *The Duchess of Malfi*.

Webster's choice of a documented Italian record of Giovanna d'Aragona, the historical Duchess of Amalfi, and Antonio Bologna as his principal source had two benefits: first, it offered, as Italian stories often did, highly dramatic elements: secret marriage that defied the boundaries of class; discovery by spies; flight disguised as a pilgrimage; capture by the Duchess's two enraged brothers, one the Duke of Calabria, the other a prince of the church; the strangling of their sister and her younger children; and eventual murder of her lover by a hired bravo. The second benefit was less obvious, but real: criticism of rulers could be dangerous if the play were set in England and appeared to criticize King James, whether directly or indirectly. In the event, the only contemporary criticism of which we are aware came from a Catholic chaplain, Orazio Busino, who believed the play attacked Catholicism to please its Protestant audience, as we shall see below. Webster's personal knowledge included the bellman and exhortation to repentance provided by his own parish church (as a result of an endowment that Webster's father signed as a witness), and almost certainly the funeral effigy of Prince Henry, whose death occurred in late 1612 at the time Webster was writing Act IV, with its wax effigies. Presumably Webster also had direct knowledge of the legal issues surrounding marriage '*per verba de praesenti*' (I.i.479; explained in Swinburne's *Treatise of Spousals* below). In *The Duchess of Malfi* he mingles diametrically opposed social attitudes to the remarriage of widows (at all, let alone secretly) that are clearly differentiated in his two prose 'characters' of widows published a year or so after the first performance of *The Duchess of Malfi*.

Webster also read widely, including Goulart's description of lycanthropy, Sidney's *Arcadia*, and his major source for this play, the account of the Duchess and Antonio in Painter's *Palace of Pleasure*. We can see how painstakingly Webster will take a phrase or brief passage from the source, and transform it to his purposes as if he were selecting fragments from which to create a new and startling mosaic.

In the various selections that follow, spelling and some punctuation have been modernized.

From the journal of Orazio Busino, chaplain to the Venetian ambassador in London, 7 February 1618

On another occasion they showed a cardinal in all his grandeur, in the formal robes appropriate to his station, splendid and rich, with his train in attendance, having an altar erected on the stage, where he pretended to make a prayer, organizing a procession; and then they produced him in public with a harlot on his knee. They showed him giving poison to one of his sisters, in a question of honour. Moreover he goes to war, first laying down his cardinal's habit on the altar, with the help of his chaplains, with great ceremoniousness; finally he has his sword bound on and dons the soldier's sash with so much panache you could not imagine it better done. And all this was acted in condemnation of the grandeur of the Church, which they despise and which in this kingdom they hate to the death.

From a 'Charitable Deed' (8 July 1605) recording an endowment of £50 from Robert Dowe of the Merchant Taylors' Company to the parish of St Sepulchre Without Newgate to provide for a bellman to visit prisoners awaiting execution at Newgate, witnessed by John Webster Sr., father of the dramatist (cited from Charles M. Clode, *The Early History of the Guild of Merchant Taylors* [London, 1888])

... about the hour of ten of the clock, in the quiet of the night next before every execution day, [the bellman is] to go unto Newgate, there to stand so near the window as he can where the condemned prisoners do lie in the dungeon the night before they shall be executed, and with a handbell ... give there twelve solemn tolls with double strokes. And then after a good pause to deliver with a loud and audible voice (his face towards the prisoners' window), to the end the poor condemned souls may give good care and be the better stirred up to watchfulness and prayer, certain words of exhortation and prayer ... and then he shall toll his bell again.

From A *Treatise of Spousals, or Matrimonial Contracts*, by Henry Swinburne (1686; written prior to 1624)

First and principally spousals be either *de futuro*, of that which is to come, or else *de praesenti*, of that which is present. Spousals *de futuro* are a mutual promise or covenant of marriage to be had *afterwards*. ... Spousals *de praesenti* are a mutual promise or contract of *present* matrimony; as when a man doth say to the woman, 'I do take thee to my wife', and she then answereth, 'I do take thee to my husband.'…Here is…a present and perfect consent, the which alone maketh matrimony, without either public solemnization or carnal copulation; for neither is the one nor the other of the essence of matrimony, but consent only.…When the parties do contract spousals by words of *present time*, as, 'I take thee to my wife'…by these kind of words, uttered by either party, are contracted spousals *de praesenti*, which kind of spousals…are in truth and substance very matrimony indissoluble.

From John Webster's *New Characters,* contributed to the sixth edition (1615) of Sir Thomas Overbury's *Characters* (technically Overbury's postumously published poem *A Wife,* to which were added 'many witty Characters', including thirty-two by Webster)

A Virtuous Widow

Is the palm tree, that thrives not after the supplanting of her husband. For her children's sake she first marries, for she married that she might have children, and for their sakes she marries no more. She is like the purest gold, only employed for princes' medals: she never receives but one mans impression. The large jointure moves her not, titles of honour cannot sway her. To change her name were, she thinks, to commit a sin should make her ashamed of her husband's calling. She thinks she hath traveled all the world in one man; the rest of her time therefore she directs to heaven. Her main superstition is she thinks her husband's ghost would walk should she not perform his will: she would do it, were there no Prerogative Court. She gives much to pious uses, without any hope to merit by them; and as one diamond fashions another, so is she wrought into works of charity with the dust or ashes of her husband. She lives to see herself full of time: being so necessary for earth, God calls her not to heaven, till she be very aged. And even then, though her natural strength fail her, she stands like an ancient pyramid, which the less it grows to mans eye the nearer it reaches to heaven. This latter chastity of hers is more grave and reverend than that ere she was married, for in it is neither hope, nor longing, nor feare, nor jealousy. She ought to be a mirror for our youngest dames to dress themselves by when she is fullest of wrinkles. No calamity can now come near her, for in suffering the loss of her husband she accounts all the rest trifles. She hath laid his dead body in the worthiest monument that can be – she hath buried it in her own heart. To conclude, she is a relict that without any superstition in the world, though she will not be kissed, yet may be reverenced.

An Ordinary Widow

Is like the herald's hearse cloth: she serves to many funerals with a very little altering the colour. The end of her husband begins in tears, and the end of her tears begins in a husband. She uses to [frequents] cunning women to know how many husbands she shall have, and never marries without the consent of six midwives. Her chiefest pride is in the multitude of her suitors; and by them she gains, for one serves to draw on another, and with one at last she shoots out another, as boys do pellets in elder guns. She commends to them a single life, as horse coursers doe their jades, to put them away. Her fancy is to one of the biggest of the guard, but knighthood makes her draw in a weaker bow. Her servants, or kinsfolk, are the trumpeters that summon any to this combat. By them she gains much credit, but loseth it again in the old proverb, *Fama est mendax* ['*Fame is false*']. If she live to be thrice married, she seldom fails to cozen her second husband's creditors. A churchman she dare not venture upon, for she hath heard widows complain of dilapidations; nor a soldier, though he have candle-rents in the City, for his estate may be subject to fire; very seldom a lawyer, without he show his exceeding great practice, and can make her case the better; but a knight with the old rent may do much, for a great coming in is all in all with a widow – ever provided that most part of her plate and jewels (before the wedding) lie concealed with her scrivener. Thus, like a too ripe apple, she falls of herself; but he that hath her is lord but of a filthy purchase, for the title is cracked. Lastly, while she is a widow, observe ever she is no mourning woman: the evening a good fire and sack may make her listen to a husband, and if ever she be made sure, 'tis upon a full stomach to bedward.

From Simon Goulart's *Admirable and Memorable Histories,* translated by Edward Grimeston (1607)

There be *Lycanthropes* in whom the melancholic humour doth so rule as they imagine themselves to be transformed into wolves. This disease ... is a kind of melancholy, but very black and vehement: for such as are touched therewith ... counterfeit wolves in all manner of things, and all night do nothing but run into churchyards, and about graves ... I have observed one of these melancholic *Lycanthropes*. ... He carried then upon his shoulders the whole thigh and the leg of a dead man. ... There was also ... a country man near unto *Pavia*, in the year 1541. ... He did constantly affirm that he was a wolf, and that there was no other difference, but that wolves were commonly hairy without, and he was betwixt the skin and the flesh. ... Such as are afflicted with that disease ... have the imagination so impaired and hurt ... by some particular power of Satan, they seem wolves and not men. ...

From *The Palace of Pleasure* by William Painter (1567), translated and adapted from *Histoires Tragiques* by Francois de Belleforest (1565), itself derived from the *Novelle* by Matteo Bandello (1554)

In the following extracts from Painter's Palace of Pleasure, *two main elements are in play: first, the historical facts, and second, moral injunctions from the writer. The ominous introductory section stresses the duty of aristocrats and rulers to set a good example, with women regarded as having a special obligation to be modest and chaste.*

THE DUCHESS OF MALFI

The Unfortunate Marriage of a Gentleman called Antonio Bologna, with the Duchess of Malfi, and the pitiful death of them both.

The greater honour and authority men have in this world, and the greater their estimation is, the more sensible and notorious are the faults by them committed, and the greater is their slander. ... Wherefore it behoveth the noble, and such as have charge of commonwealth, to live an honest life, and bear their port upright, that none have cause to take ill example upon discourse of their deeds and naughty [worthless, despicable] life. And above all, that modesty ought to be kept by women, whom as their race, noble birth, authority, and name maketh them more famous, even so their virtue, honesty, chastity, and continency more praiseworthy. ... Thus I say, because a woman being as it were the image of sweetness, courtesy, and shamefastness,

so soon as she steppeth out of the right tract, and leaveth the smell
of her duty and modesty, besides the denigration of her honour,
thrusteth herself into infinite troubles and causeth the ruin of such
which should be honoured and praised, if women's allurement solic-
ited them not to folly. ...

*Webster makes Antonio less prominent than his source, but retains surprising
detail, such as Antonio's time in France, and his horsemanship. And where
Painter's Duchess is blameworthy for her 'shameful lusts', Webster's is more
complex and sympathetic.*

In that very time then lived a gentleman of Naples called Antonio
Bologna, who having been Master of Household to Frederick of
Aragon, sometime King of Naples, after the French had expelled
those of Aragon out of that city the said Bologna retired into France.
The gentleman had a passing number of good graces ... and for riding
and managing of great horse he had not his fellow in Italy. ... But what!
It is impossible to eschew that which the heavens have determined
upon us. ... Even so it chanced to this Neapolitan gentleman, for in the
very same place where he attained his advancement, he received also
his diminution and decay; and by that house which preferred him to
what he had, he was deprived both of his estate and life. ...

The Duchess of Malfi thought to entreat him that he would serve
her in that office which he served the king. ... This lady was a widow,
but a passing fair gentlewoman, fine and very young, having a
young son under her guard and keeping, left by the deceased Duke
her husband, together with the Duchy, the inheritance of her child.
Now consider – her personage being such, her easy life and deli-
cate bringing up, and daily seeing the youthly trade and manner of
courtiers' life – whether she felt herself pricked with any desire, which
burned her heart the more incessantly, as the flames were hidden and
covert; from the outward show whereof she stayed herself so well as
she could. But she ... rather esteemed the proof of marriage than ... to
incur the exchange of lovers, as many unshamefast [unchaste] strum-
pets do. ... So her mishap began already to spin the thread which
choked the air and breath of her unhappy life.

Ye have heard before that Master Bologna was one of the wisest
and most perfect gentlemen that the land of Naples that time
brought forth, and for his beauty, proportion, galantness, valiance,
and good grace, without comparison. ... Who then could blame this
fair princess if (pressed with desire of match, to remove the ticklish

instigations of her wanton flesh, and having in her presence a man so wise) she did set her mind on him, or fantasy to marry him? ... The Duchess became extremely in love with the master of her house. In such wise as before all men, she spared not to praise the great perfections wherewith he was enriched, whom she desired to be altogether hers. ... She could not tell what way to hold, to [have] him understand her heart and affection. She feared to discover the same unto him, doubting either of some fond and rigorous answer, or of revealing of her mind to him whose presence pleased her more than all the men of the world. 'Alas,' said she, 'shall a lady of such blood as I am be constrained to sue, where all other be required by importunate instance of their suitors? ... I think we be the daily slaves of the fond and cruel fantasy of those tyrants, which say they have puissance over us; and that straining our will to their tyranny, we be still bound to the chain like the galley slave. No, no, Bologna shall be my husband, for of a friend I purpose to make him my loyal and lawful husband, meaning thereby not to offend God and men together. ...'

Thus the Duchess founded her enterprise, determining to marry her household master. ... Vanquished with love and impatience, she was forced to break off silence, and to assure herself in him, rejecting fear conceived of shame, to make her way to pleasure, which she lusted more than marriage, the same serving her but for a mask and coverture to hide her follies and shameless lusts, for which she did the penance that her folly deserved. ... Upon a time [she] sent for him up into her chamber, as commonly she did for the affairs and matters of her house, and taking him aside unto a window, having prospect into a garden, she. ... took Bologna by the hand and, dissembling what she thought, used this or such like language: ... 'you know and see how I am a widow. ... Wherefore I am resolved, without respite or delay, to choose some well-qualitied and renowned gentleman, that hath more virtue than riches, of good fame and bruit [report], to the intent I may make him my lord, spouse, and husband. ... Thus much I say, and it is the sum of all my secrets, wherein I pray your council and advice. ...'

Seeing her friend rapt with the passion and standing still unmoveable through fear ... she said thus unto him: 'Signor Antonio. ... think me not ... so foolish to think you to be so indiscreet, but that you have marked my countenance and manner, and thereby have known that I have been more affectioned to you than to any other. For that cause,' said she, straining him by the hand very lovingly, and with cheerful colour in her face, 'I swear unto you, and do promise that if you so think meet, it shall be none other but yourself whom I will have and desire to take to husband and lawful spouse....'

The gentleman, hearing such sudden talk, and the assurance of that which he most wished for, albeit he saw the danger extreme whereunto he launched himself by espousing this great lady, and the enemies he should get by entering such alliance (notwithstanding building upon vain hope, and thinking at length that the choler of the Aragon brother would pass away if they understood the marriage), determined to pursue the purpose and not to refuse that great preferment being so prodigally offered, for which cause he answered his lady in this manner: 'If...till this time I delayed to open that which now I discover unto you, I beseech you, madam, to impute it to the greatness of your estate, and to the duty of my calling and office in your house, being not seemly for a servant to talk of such secrets with his lady and mistress.... Now for so much as of your motion, grace, courtesy and liberality the same is offered, and that it pleaseth you to accept me for yours, I humbly beseech you to dispose of me not as husband, but of one which is, and shall be your servant forever, and such as is more ready to obey, than you to command. It resteth now, madam, to consider how, and in what wise our affairs are to be directed that, things being in assurance, you may so live without peril and bruit of slanderous tongues, as your good fame and honest port may continue without spot or blemish.'

Behold the first act of the tragedy, and the provision of the fare which afterwards sent them both to their grave, who immediately gave their mutual faith.... And for the present time they passed the same in words, for ratification whereof they went to bed together.

The 'first act' is indeed Webster's first act, but he chooses and reworks what follows into his own new plot and character elements – especially Bosola's spying for Ferdinand. In the play the Duchess makes the decisions for a weak Antonio, and Cariola, far from planning the pilgrimage to Loretto, objects to it (just as Painter does).

But the pain in the end was greater than the pleasure.... For albeit their marriage was secret...and that Bologna more oft held the state of the steward of the house by day than of lord of the same, and by night supplied that place, yet in the end, the thing was perceived which they desired to be closely kept. And as it is impossible to till and culture a fertile ground but that the same must yield some fruit, even so the

Duchess after many pleasures (being ripe and plentiful) became with child, which at the first stunned the married couple. Nevertheless, the same so well was provided for, as the first childbed was kept secret, and none did know thereof. ... The Duchess being great with child again and delivered of a girl, the business of the same was not so secretly done, but that it was discovered. And it sufficed not that the bruit was noised through Naples, but that the sound flew further off.

As each man doth know that rumour hath many mouths ... so that babbling fool carried the news of that second childbed to the ears of the Cardinal of Aragon, the Duchess' brother, being then at Rome. ... They were extremely wroth with this happened slander and with the dishonest fame which the Duchess had gotten throughout Italy, yet far greater was their sorrow and grief, for that they did not know what he was that so courteously was allied to their house and in their love had increased their lineage. And therefore, swelling with despite and rapt with fury to see themselves so defamed by one of their blood, they purposed by all means whatsoever it cost them to know the lucky lover that had so well tilled the Duchess their sister's field. ...

The Duchess' court being in this trouble, she did continually perceive in her house her brothers' men to mark her countenance, and to note those that came thither to visit her, and to whom she used greatest familiarity ... they purposed to change their estate for a time, by yielding truce to their pleasures. ... Bologna was a wise and provident personage, fearing to be surprised. ... And as they were secretly in their chamber together, he used these or such like words: 'Madam ... You see the solemn watch and guard which the servants of the lords your brothers do within your house, and the suspicion which they have conceived by reason of your second childbed, and by what means they labour truly to know how your affairs proceed and things do pass. I fear not death where your service may be advanced ... but be assured that a great band, and the same well armed, will set upon me. I pray you, madam, suffer me to retire for a time, for I am assured that when I am absent, they will never soil their hands, or imbrue their swords in your blood. ... And therefore I am determined to go from Naples ... and from thence to Ancona until it pleaseth God to mitigate the rage of your brethren, and recover their good wills to consent to our marriage. ...'

She embraced him very amorously, and he kissed her ... sorrowful beyond measure so to leave her whom he loved. ... In the end, fearing

that the Aragon espials would come and perceive them in those privi-
ties, Bologna took his leave, and bade his lady and spouse farewell.

And thus was the second act of this tragical history, to see a fugi-
tive husband secretly to marry, especially her upon whom he ought
not so much as to look but with fear and reverence.... True it is that
marriages be done in Heaven and performed in earth, but that saying
may not be applied to fools, which govern themselves by carnal
desires, whose scope is but pleasure, and the reward many times
equal to their folly. Shall I be of opinion that a household servant
ought to solicit, nay rather suborn, the daughter of his lord without
punishment, or that a vile and abject person dare to mount upon a
princess' bed? No, no; policy requireth order in all, and each wight
ought to be matched according to their quality.....

Come we again then to sir Bologna, who...repaired to Ancona,
a city of the patrimony of the Roman Church, whither he carried
his two children which he had of the Duchess....There he hired a
house for his train, and for those that waited upon his wife, who in
the meantime was in great care.... Perceiving that her belly began to
swell and grow to the time of her delivery....the gentlewoman of her
chamber...gave her this advice:...'If your sorrow be so great over sir
Bologna, and if you fear your childbed will be descried, why seek
you not means to attempt some voyage for covering of the fact, to
beguile the eyes of them which so diligently do watch you?...Let your
household understand that you have made a vow to visit the holy
temple of our Lady of Loretto (a famous place of pilgrimage in Italy),
and...from thence you shall take your journey to sojourn at Ancona
whither, before you depart, you shall send your moveables and plate,
with such money as you shall think necessary. And afterwards God
will perform the rest, and through his holy mercy will guide and
direct all your affairs.'

The Duchess, hearing the maiden speak those words and amazed
of her sudden invention, could not forbear to embrace and kiss her,
blessing the hour wherein she was born....It was not sufficient for
this foolish woman to take a husband, more to glut her libidinous
appetite than for other occasion, except she added to her sin, another
execrable impiety, making holy places and duties of devotion to be as
it were the ministers of her folly.

The Duchess...the morrow after her arrival to Ancona assembled
all her train in the hall, of purpose no longer to keep secret that sir

Bologna was her husband, and that already she had had two children by him and again was great with child. ...

This was the preparative of the catastrophe and bloody end of this tragedy. ... These news reported to the Cardinal and his brother, it may be considered how grievously they took the same. ... 'Ha!' said the Prince, transported with choler and driven into deadly fury ... 'what a great abomination is this, that a gentlewoman of such a house as ours is hath forgotten her estate, and the greatness of her alliance, besides the nobility of her deceased husband, with the hope of the toward youth of the Duke her son and our nephew. ... What abuse have they committed under title of marriage, which was so secretly done, as their children do witness their filthy embracements, but their promise of faith was made in open air, and serveth for a cloak and vizard for their most filthy whoredom. And what if marriage was concluded: be we of so little respect as the carrion beast would not vouchsafe to advertise us of her intent? Or is Bologna a man worthy to be allied or mingled with the royal blood of Aragon and Castile? No no, be he never so good a gentleman, his race agreeth not with kingly state. But I make to God a vow, that never will I take one sound and restful sleep until I have dispatched that infamous fact from our blood, and that the caitiff whoremonger be used according to his desert.'

The Cardinal also was out of quiet, grinding his teeth together ... promising no better usage to their Bologna than his younger brother did. And the better to entrap them both ... they sent to the ... Cardinal of Mantua, then legate for Pope Julius the second at Ancona, at whose hands they enjoyed such friendship as Bologna and all his family were commanded speedily to avoid the city. ... The Cardinal night nor day did sleep, and his brother still did wait to perform his oath of revenge. ...

These two unfortunate, husband and wife, were chased from all places. ... One of the train afar off did see a troop of horsemen galloping towards their company, which by their countenance showed no sign of peace or amity at all, which made them consider that it was some ambush of their enemies. ... The good lady said unto him: 'Sir, for all the joys and pleasures which you can do me, for God's sake save yourself and the little infant next you, who can well endure the galloping of the horse. For sure I am that you being out of our company, we shall not need to fear any hurt. But if you do tarry, you will be the cause of the ruin and overthrow of us all, and receive thereby no profit or advantage. Take this purse therefore, and save yourself, attending better fortune in time to come.'

The poor gentleman Bologna, knowing that his wife had pronounced reason, and perceiving that it was impossible from that time forth that she or her train could escape their hands, taking leave of her and kissing his children, not forgetting the money which she offered unto him, willed his servants to save themselves by such means as they thought best. So, giving spurs unto his horse he began to flee amain, and his eldest son, seeing his father gone, began to follow in like sort. And so for that time they two were saved by breaking of the intended ill luck like to light upon them. ... In the meantime the horsemen were approached near the Duchess, who seeing that Bologna had saved himself, very courteously began to speak unto the lady ... 'Madam, we be commanded by the lords your brethren to conduct you home unto your house. ...'

But she was greatly deceived ... for so soon as these gallants had conducted her into the kingdom of Naples, to one of the castles of her son, she was committed to prison with her children, and she also that was the secretary of her unfortunate marriage. Till this time Fortune was contented to proceed with indifferent quiet against those lovers, but henceforth ye shall hear the issue of their little prosperous love, and how pleasure, having blinded them, never forsook them until it had given them the overthrow. ...

Painter describes the deaths of the Duchess and Antonio relatively simply. Webster adds the stage horror of waxwork hands and bodies, of madmen, lycanthropia and disguise, and of the emotion around madness, revenge, and salvation. He also adjusts details, for instance making Cariola's death not merely a cry for justice, but an ironic counterpoint to the way the Duchess accepts death.

That miserable princess ... seeing herself a prisoner in the company of her little children and well-beloved maiden, patiently lived in hope to see her brethren appeased, comforting herself for the escape of her husband out of the hands of his mortal foes. But her assurance was changed into an horrible fear ... when certain days after her imprisonment, her gaoler came in and said unto her: 'Madam, I do advise you henceforth to consider upon your conscience, for so much as I suppose that even this very day your life shall be taken from you.'

... 'Alas,' said she, 'is it possible that my brethren should so far forget themselves as, for a fact nothing prejudicial unto them, cruelly to put to death their innocent sister, and to imbrue the memory of their fact in the blood of one which never did offend them?' ... Two or three of the ministers which had taken her ... came in and said unto her: 'Now, madam, make ready yourself to go to God, for behold your hour is come.'

'Praised be that God,' said she, 'for the wealth and woe which it pleaseth him to send us. But I beseech you, my friends, to have pity upon these little children and innocent creatures. Let them not feel the smart which I am assured my brethren bear against their poor unhappy father.'

'Well, well, madam,' said they, 'we will convey them to such a place as they shall not want.'

'I also recommend unto you,' quoth she, 'this poor maiden, and entreat her well in consideration of her good service done to the unfortunate Duchess of Malfi.'

As she had ended those words, the two ruffians did put a cord about her neck, and strangled her. The maiden, seeing the piteous tragedy commenced upon her mistress, cried out amain and cursed the cruel malice of those tormenters, and besought God to be witness of the same, and crying out upon his divine majesty, she besought him to bend his judgement against them which causeless (being no magistrates), had killed such innocent creatures. 'Reason it is,' said one of the tyrants, 'that thou be partaker of the joy of thy mistress' innocency, sith thou hast been so faithful a minister, and messenger of her follies.' And suddenly caught her by the hair of the head, and instead of a carcanet placed a rope about her neck. 'How now!' quoth she, 'is this the promised faith which you made unto my lady?' But those words flew into the air with her soul, in company of the miserable Duchess.

But hearken now the most sorrowful scene of all the tragedy. ... The Aragon brethren meant hereby nothing else but to root out the whole name and race of Bologna. And therefore, the two ministers of iniquity did like murder and slaughter upon those two tender babes as they committed upon their mother, not without some motion of horror for doing of an act so detestable.

Only at the end does Painter introduce Delio and Bosola; the central role Webster creates for Bosola is perhaps his greatest development of the story, and renders impossible the simple morality (though still ambiguous in its oscillation between moral lesson and misfortune) of Painter's conclusion.

In the time of these murders, the unfortunate lover kept himself at Milan with his son. ... Delio ... knowing the gentleman to be husband to the deceased Duchess of Malfi came unto him and, taking him aside, said: 'Sir, ... I of late was in company with a nobleman of Naples ... who told me that he had a special charge to kill you. ..... Moreover I have worse tidings to tell you, which are that the Duchess your wife is dead by violent hand in prison, and the most part of them that were in her company. ... '

In the meantime, the cruel spirit of the Aragon brethren were not yet appeased with the former murders, but needs must finish the last act of Bologna his tragedy by loss of his life, to keep his wife and children company so well in another world, as he was united with them in love in this frail and transitory passage. ... It chanced that a Lombard ... inveigled with covetousness, and hired for ready money, practised the death of the Duchess' poor husband. This bloody beast was called Daniel de Bozola that had charge of a certain band of footmen in Milan. This new Judas and assured man-queller, within certain days after knowing that Bologna oftentimes repaired to hear service at the church and convent of St Francis, secretly conveyed himself in ambush, hard beside the church of St James whither he came (being accompanied with a certain troop of soldiers), to assail the unfortunate Bologna, who was sooner slain than he was able to think upon defence. ...

Behold here the noble fact of a Cardinal, and what savour it hath of Christian purity: to commit a slaughter for a fact done many years past upon a poor gentleman which never thought him hurt. Is this the sweet observation of the Apostles, of whom they vaunt themselves to be the successors and followers? ... Such end had the unfortunate marriage of him, which ought to have contented himself with that degree and honour that he had acquired by his deeds and glory of his virtues. ... You see the miserable discourse of a princess' love that was not very wise, and of a gentleman that had forgotten his estate, which ought to serve for a looking glass to them which be over hardy ... where they ought to maintain themselves in reputation, and bear the title of well-advised: foreseeing their ruin to be example to all posterity, as may be seen by the death of Bologna, and of all them which sprang of him, and of his unfortunate spouse his lady and mistress.

4 Key Productions and Performances

Peggy Ashcroft in 1945 and 1960

When *The Duchess of Malfi* opened at the Haymarket Theatre in London, on 18 April 1945, with leading British classical actors, it was the first major production since the nineteenth century. From about 1850 to 1875 the play had been a starring vehicle on both sides of the Atlantic for actresses playing the Duchess in a heavily cut and melodramatic adaptation that allowed her to display an acting range from aristocratic coquetry to grand tragedy. But since then it had dropped from the repertoire, apart from a few experimental and university productions. Furthermore, Webster's critical reputation had been undermined by William Archer's 1893 dismissal of him as 'not ... a great dramatist, but ... a great poet who wrote haphazard dramatic or melodramatic romances for [a] semi-barbarous public'; by George Bernard Shaw's pronouncement that he was the 'Tussaud laureate' (referring to the grisly waxworks at Madame Tussaud's museum); and by T. S. Eliot's similarly morbid dictum that Webster 'saw the skull beneath the skin' (see p. 133). The omens were not auspicious.

The Haymarket Theatre production of 1945

Against the odds, the Haymarket production was a theatrical and critical success, and indeed the director, George Rylands, was invited to repeat his success on Broadway the following year (though rewriting by Bertolt Brecht and W. H. Auden, and the difficulty the German actress Elizabeth Bergner encountered with English verse speaking contributed to a vastly less satisfactory result). Rylands had played the role of the Duchess himself as a student at Cambridge University in 1924, and subsequently directed the play for the same university-based group, the Marlowe Society. He brought both theatrical and scholarly experience to the production, and cut relatively little of Webster's text compared to many modern directors. He was somewhat old-fashioned as a director, and certainly there were recognizably romantic and melodramatic elements in his approach; nonetheless, he created a landmark production for both performance and critical history of the play.

A sense of the Italian Renaissance setting, and of nineteenth-century stage pictorialism, was retained in painted pillars and backdrop landscapes, but they were deliberately rough impressions rather than realistic. Similarly, the bare two-level stage space acknowledged early modern conventions of multiple contexts, such as Cariola watching from slightly above as the Duchess and Antonio exchanged wedding vows in I.i, or the courtiers observing the Duchess in the apricot scene (II.i). Stage lighting often created shadows that made the space seem one of 'sombre magnificence'. Within this setting the rich and heavy Renaissance costumes added to the sense of historical period, and the downfall of the Duchess could be charted by the gradual diminution of her heavy jewellery.

Peggy Ashcroft, already a leading Shakespearean actress (she played Ophelia and Titania in the same season), followed the traditional interpretation of the character, from sparkling vivacity early on, to tender warmth and happiness married to Antonio, and finally a noble purity and dignity of suffering as catastrophe approached. She prepared herself for death kneeling, wearing a cross at her breast, and with her palms turned outward in the manner of a medieval Christian martyr. Some critics longed for more tragic grandeur and majesty, but all praised her noble simplicity.

Playing opposite Ashcroft as her twin brother Ferdinand was another great Shakespearean actor, John Gielgud. Two aspects of his performance stood out, and were related: his wild, wolvish brainsickness, and his clearly incestuous attraction to his sister Duchess. While incest had been hinted at in earlier twentieth-century productions, this was the first to make it a major element of the character, and was a novelty for most audiences and critics. As a result, his frantic lycanthropia seemed to arise out of the neurotic Freudian longing he only half understood. Gielgud, who regarded the character as 'entirely evil', conveyed an utter ruthlessness; the famous critic Kenneth Tynan, in *He That Plays the King* (London, 1950), p. 42, recalled 'the awful finality' of Ferdinand's 'I shall never see thee more' (III.ii.141). And although the Cardinal was generally regarded as too gracious and insufficiently villainous, the pair of brothers together conducted a formidable assault on the Duchess that allowed her transcendent dignity to shine the brighter.

One of the triumphs of the production was the centrality of Bosola, 'a stout, conscience-stricken intelligencer, brooding over the corruption of the time with a kind of dark, angry relish' who appeared to 'look deeply into wickedness with the paradoxical desire of seeing good blossom there' (*The Times*). Cecil Trouncer played the role with great gusto, but it was the intelligence he gave Bosola that was crucial to the general reassessment of Webster that this production introduced.

A critical contextual element of this reassessment was the date the production opened in London: 18 April 1945. The page of *The Times* on which the production of *The Duchess of Malfi* was reviewed the next day also carried the first photographs of the Nazi death camps that the Allied armies had just reached and liberated. Juxtaposition with images of emaciated corpses from Nordhausen and Buchenwald stacked on wagons lent a new topicality and seriousness to Webster's tragedy.

The Shakespeare Memorial Theatre Company at the Aldwych, 1960

Peggy Ashcroft played the role again in 1960 for the opening production, at their new London theatre, of the Shakespeare Memorial Company from Stratford (soon to be renamed the Royal Shakespeare Company, the RSC). It is instructive to look at similarities and differences.

Donald McWhinnie, an experienced radio director, was praised for achieving a great clarity and intelligence of speech, and natural motivation. This focus on psychological realism of thought and speech may have led to the cutting of some of the least realist parts of the play, such as the dumb show of the arming of the Cardinal in III.iv, but the stage setting was far from realist. It was relatively bare and, unusually for the time, thrust out beyond the proscenium arch.

A few enormous 'super-props' such as a twelve foot high (nearly four metres) throne for the Cardinal, and a towering canopied bed for the Duchess in III.ii, dominated the bare stage in emblematic fashion. But they were also used to aid psychologically motivated acting. For instance, a vast fountain set the scene for the start of the play, providing a visual emblem for Antonio's opening speech about justice or corruption at court being akin to a fountain; but Antonio entered hot from the tilting, wrung out his handkerchief in the fountain to mop his brow, and gave the impression that the idea of the fountain as an image arose from his proximity to one. The production thus caught the duality of Webster's baroque stylization of language and spectacle combined with intensely psychological reality of feeling. However, this did not extend to retaining the sections of the play about war and politics, so the focus became primarily on the personal and domestic, and especially on the Duchess herself.

Ashcroft's interpretation of the Duchess was at the centre of the production, and critics who had seen both productions noted the increase in intelligence, subtlety, and authority with which she played. Despite the director intending her to be 'wilful and headstrong', however, she preserved the restrained dignity of the earlier production. The same pattern of early vivacity developing into radiant tenderness in her marriage to Antonio was retained, and highest praise was given to the depth of feeling with which she endowed the noble Duchess. She died still asserting her own pride in 'I am Duchess of Malfi still' (IV.ii.141) and was the very model of a Christian heroine secure in her own integrity, but dissatisfaction continued to be expressed about her portraying the Duchess as too genteel and restrained to generate fully tragic terror and pity.

Although Eric Porter's Ferdinand did not thrill critics in the way Gielgud had done in 1945, he displayed a more complex set of motivations. His lycanthropic madness appeared from the first moment he appeared; and while an incestuous passion was hinted at, power and avarice were more evident driving forces. And in this production the Cardinal, played by Max Adrian, was a stronger force: icy authority combined with a sour cynicism. In addition, his lechery with a vigorously sensual Julia implied a further unrecognized brotherly attraction to incest, since Julia's red hair exactly matched that of the Duchess.

The great disappointment of the production was Bosola. Patrick Wymark was a comic actor, and although he easily attained the essential comic rapport the character must establish with the audience, he failed to portray the intelligence or anguish of the 1945 Bosola. However, the Duchess's radiant warmth and nobility dominated the play until her death late in Act IV, and the speed and ensemble acting of Act V saved it from disintegrating into laughter, making this one of the very few productions to succeed despite a weak Bosola.

Conceptual theatre: Philip Prowse as director/designer in 1975 and 1985

The Glasgow Citizens production, 1975

Philip Prowse is a designer turned director, and his first production of *The Duchess of Malfi*, at the Citizens Theatre, Glasgow in 1975, displayed his trademark reliance on visual spectacle to communicate his conceptual vision of the play. The set was a great terraced pyramid, a shrine to Death, who sat, black-robed in a golden mask, enthroned at the top. Skeletons in court costume, or in some cases ecclesiastical vestments and mitres, doubled the apparent size of the cast, and provided both an atmosphere and critique relating to death. Black and gold were the predominant colours of the set and costumes, giving an effect of oppressive decadence; one critic described the set as a 'baroque mausoleum' (Christopher Small, *Glasgow Herald*). The terraced steps became a literal equivalent of Fortune's wheel, or of Bosola's image of the hospital 'where this man's head lies at that man's foot' (I.i.67), when Julia rolled down them in death. Costumes were very constricting – rigid squared stomachers, highly wrought ruffs – and makeup white in a way that was frequently seen in 1970s productions, emphasizing the rigidities and constrictions not only surrounding the Duchess at court, but also hierarchical societies more widely. Class was evident in movement, with lower status characters bowing, moving stiffly backwards from rulers, and often frozen in tableaux.

This apparent social concern was limited, however; much of the ethical, military, religious, and political reference in the text was cut in order to simplify the play. So too were emotional and ethical ironies and progressions; for instance, the Duchess's impulse towards suicide in IV.i.

Excising the complexities of Webster's text was essential to give priority to the visual metaphor of Death presiding over the Theatre of the World. All the characters were looking for death/Death, consciously or not, in order to give meaning to their lives. There was no gaiety at the start, nor were Antonio and Delio allowed to create a moral framework by which to view the main characters. To emphasize the existentialist bent of the production, the silent figure of Death would descend from time to time to hold open a book of *sententiae* (see pp. 13–14) for a character to read from (thus neatly underlining what often seems to be Webster's authorial comment in these passages), or to physically direct characters towards moments of fateful decision (for instance, Bosola talked briefly with Death before killing the Duchess in IV.ii, and Death held the Cardinal captive as Bosola threatened him in V.v).

The pace of the production was slow and deliberate, punctuated by ominous whispers, footsteps, and screams. The lighting suddenly changed to white when Bosola learned of the Duchess's secret marriage; he would now search out the truth. But at the end, when he tried to reach the veiled ghost of the Duchess (now standing at the top beside Death), he failed, and knew he had failed. This unattainable vision brought the production very close to the melodramatic ending written for the nineteenth-century theatre, though then it had been Ferdinand trying to reach her.

Act V of the play was by this time notorious for its difficulty: the absence of the Duchess, and the multiple deaths at the end, create problems for directors in maintaining tragic intensity and in avoiding unwanted laughter at the final blood-bath. Prowse failed to prevent laughter as character after character expired in gouts of blood (Bosola upside down vomiting blood), but tried to maintain some thematic unity by the presence of the ghost of the Duchess as mentioned above.

The Duchess was played by Suzanne Bertish in a manner that Donald McWhinnie had failed to persuade Peggy Ashcroft to adopt fifteen years earlier, as her brothers' sister – wilful, stubborn, and passionate. She was playfully possessive in the wooing scene at the end of I.i (of an immature and petulant Antonio), and bejeweled and defiant in death. The production did not permit Christian serenity, and a noble death in a darkly existential world is exceptionally difficult to convey.

The dominant character in this production (apart from the mute figure of Death) was Bosola, who was highly praised for capturing the bitterness and anguish of the man as well as his criminality. He always carried a book. The director did not encourage a realist 'through line' in characterization, but rather sudden jumps of attitude in keeping with the text. Thus Bosola was simply earning his money until the Duchess died; then, and only then, did he regret killing her. After that a slight stutter emphasized his inner conflict. Allen Wright saw him as 'appalled by the depths to which he has descended' (*Scotsman*).

Overall, the production was a powerful display of designer/director's theatre, using his actors as 'über-marionettes' (super-puppets) to fill out a spectacular visual metaphor of the play. It also displayed the inevitable difficulty of such productions in sustaining dramatic interest once the visual effect has been absorbed. Heavy cutting of the text was necessary in order to fit the director's vision, and therefore the result was a simplified version of Webster.

Prowse at the National Theatre, 1985

It was ironic that the first production of the newly formed actors' company within the National Theatre in London invited such a controlling designer/director as Philip Prowse to direct their first production. Just as in Glasgow, the setting and costume were the most striking elements.

The huge space of the proscenium-arch Lyttleton Theatre at the National was divided for Acts I–III by columns, sliding walls, alcoves, and glass cases – of silver chalices, figurines cradling crucifixes, relics, miniature skulls, and *memento mori* (redolently Catholic, another 'baroque mausoleum'). Acts IV and V were more austere and the space was entirely open and vast. Sharply defined lighting, including footlights to create huge shadows, added to the sinister feeling of the environment. Costuming was similarly an extension, sometimes monstrous and grotesque, of Italian baroque style. As at Glasgow, almost everyone was dressed in black, with only occasional flashes of scarlet (the Cardinal's hat; a stocking; a nosebleed or afterbirth). The Duchess had a heavy and unwieldy court dress in black and purple for her ritualistic first entry; the contrast in Acts IV and V was startling when she (and Ferdinand) appeared in white. It gave, said one critic, 'a rich, decadent, sinister, shadowy ... sense of brooding, atmospheric evil and of religion in decay' (Sheridan Morley, *Punch*). The opening sequence revealed the same strengths and limitations as the Glasgow production: amidst a clangour of (electronic) bells calling people to prayer, and with Antonio and Delio's opening ethical speeches about princes' courts cut), a rigid, ritualistic, grotesque dead march took the court across the stage in a long procession. This was later mirrored in parody by the chained entry of tortured madmen. Strangely, most of Webster's own spectacle was cut: the dumb show of arming the Cardinal in III.iv was gone entirely, and the banishment reduced to a single slap from the Cardinal. The waxwork of Antonio was dragged on in a shroud and left in a corner, and the madmen lost their song. The entire production was accompanied by the sound of bells, ticking, screeching of peacocks and rooks, and other unnerving noises.

The figure of Death was retained, but more as a cowled onlooker than presiding authority. This was more subtle than the Glasgow interpretation, and many critics thought it added a unifying feature to the play; and of course it continued to be central to Prowse's view of Webster. Death wooed the Duchess into her coffin, and at the end of the play accompanied her ghost offstage past the dead bodies. Ferdinand was the only character to acknowledge his presence, attacking him as his shadow in V.i. However, in this production Antonio rather than Bosola (or Ferdinand in the nineteenth century) crawled towards his vision of the Duchess as he died.

Although the production's style of high decadence presented a striking vision and atmosphere of death, the text and meaning of the play had, as at Glasgow, to be reduced and simplified accordingly. But unlike Glasgow there was also widespread criticism of the acting, especially inaudibility and gabbling of lines. What audiences did not know was that a number of verse sections of the text had been re-typed for the actors as prose, and this may explain at least part of what was criticized as bad verse speaking and incoherence (see pp. 14–15). Since Prowse has been reported as believing that 'the words of an author are no more important than the work of an usherette' (Charles Spencer, *Daily Telegraph*, 20 June 1991), it seems unlikely that he cared.

But the emotional impact of the play was also found lacking, particularly from the Duchess. Eleanor Bron had a reputation as a light satiric actress, not a tragedienne. Although she was glamorous and statuesque, many reviewers found her lacking in radiance, warmth, intimacy, love, and eventual tragic stature. Her lack of emotion in Act IV (she murmured 'I am Duchess of Malfi still' without conviction) meant a failure to fulfill the potential of the role. She had little of the mettlesome energy of Suzanne Bertish in the Glasgow production, nor of the passionate warmth that Peggy Ashcroft had brought to the role.

Of the other roles, Bosola made the strongest impression. Ian McKellen's scruffy costume, shorn hair, and scholar's glasses put him outside the world of the grandees. He played a diseased intellectual (cf. III.iii.41–5) with mordant cynicism, amiable to the audience. But his half-hearted Christian comfort to the Duchess was in this production unable to make his conversion to remorse and compassion even understandable, let alone convincing.

(It is worth noting that at the Canadian Stratford Shakespearean Festival in 1971 the director and designer had staged Webster's play using visual effects that Prowse would have recognized: rich and heavily appliquéed costumes that appeared encrusted in blood, a golden world already in decay; Bosola's initial costume looked as if it had been eaten away by a corrosive acid. The *coup de théâtre* was the banishment of the Duchess, in which the Cardinal was accompanied by golden-robed churchmen through a fog of candlelit sulphurous smoke in a nightmare vision of religious opulence and evil. But in this case the voluptuous spectacle was sufficiently selective to permit also a full exploration of text, emotion, and dramatic complexity.)

Emotional realism at the RSC, 1989

Four years after Philip Prowse's morbidly stylized production at the National Theatre, the RSC returned to the play for only the second time since their 1960 production with Peggy Ashcroft. And like that production, the acting of the Duchess was at the core of the play.

Unusually for any modern production the text was virtually uncut. (It ran three and a half hours; but when it moved from the Swan Theatre at Stratford in 1989 to the Pit in the Barbican Centre in

London in 1990 the arming of the Cardinal and the banishment of the Duchess in III.iv were omitted, as was the Julia–Pescara sequence in V.i).

In some respects Bill Alexander, the director, recognized the non-realist demands of the play as much as Philip Prowse had done. The opening, for instance, showed the Duchess and her two brothers framed in one of the Swan's (and later the Pit's) alcoves, but then she suddenly burst out of the tableau into an exuberant Flamenco dance. The scene proceeded with Antonio and Delio commenting on the courtiers in loud voices from opposite sides of the stage. The courtiers were oblivious to the commentary, and sometimes froze in tableau as they were discussed. The set itself was obviously theatrical, with the architectural features of the quasi-Georgian galleried Swan and the stage at both theatres a bare performance space on which were placed a few curtains and sparse large props to set the scene (a prie-dieu kneeler; a huge crucifix hanging over the lascivious Cardinal's highly sexualized meeting with Julia in II.iv; a giant lectern and book for him to poison her with in V.ii). Heavy jewels encrusted both set and costumes, offering a visual context of 'fetid opulence' (Jim Hiley, *Listener*).

Yet unlike the Prowse productions, the main focus in this production was on psychological realism, downplaying melodrama and horror in favour of exploration of character: 'charting the intellectual passage of [Webster's] doomed protagonists' (Steve Grant, *Time Out*). When Ferdinand demanded 'Why do you laugh?' (I.i.122), an utterly uneasy silence followed. He and the Cardinal were heavily hostile to the Duchess in their catechism of her about marriage, but she responded with silent mock applause after the Cardinal left. During this early part of the play Harriet Walter (a protégée and great admirer of Peggy Ashcroft) was acclaimed for her range of interpretation, and for combining 'regal dignity with a warm and roguish sexuality' (Charles Spencer, *Daily Telegraph*). Her wooing of Antonio was animated, even fun, and by the time the production got to the Pit, 'one of the most erotically charged sequences I have ever seen in a classical production' (*Listener*). But Antonio was clearly terrified at the risk (with good reason, of course). When in II.i the Duchess went into labour he desperately turned to Delio for calm advice. And after Ferdinand's visit to the Duchess in III.ii Antonio had clearly been waiting and listening behind a curtain, afraid to come in until Ferdinand left.

In that scene, after domestic happiness had been signaled by a framed tableau of the Duchess and her children with their toys, and by the warmth of the interplay between the Duchess and Antonio, she displayed both a refusal to sustain a hypocritical public face to her brother, and a genuinely loving attempt to comfort him during his frantic rage at her for remarrying without his permission. She extended her hand to him on 'Will you see my husband?' (III.ii.86) so as to lead him to Antonio; his response was ferocious rage, and he was clearly out of control by the end of his long speech at ll. 88–109, so she comforted and calmed him even as she delivered her justification ('Why might not I marry?' etc., 109–11). She was frantic with anxiety for Antonio's safety in III.v, desperate until he departed with their son to safety before Bosola returned to arrest them.

Following the single interval (see pp. 11–12) the Duchess first reacted with revulsion and violent despair, but then gradually seemed to accept her fate as curiously inevitable even if undeserved. A deep melancholy enveloped the production. Indeed, she was so attractively and realistically vulnerable that the pressures brought to bear on her in Act IV (dead man's hand; waxworks of Antonio and the children; madmen; Bosola as tomb-maker) appeared grotesque and excessive. Several critics noted the great danger in playing Webster too much in a realist mode when so many of his effects are so emblematic. Nevertheless, Walter continued to present the Duchess as thoughtful and deeply sympathetic in her sad-eyed despair, even when the horrifying but strangely religious choir of Madmen circled her menacingly. She barely had strength to affirm 'I am Duchess of Malfi still', and there was 'unbearable tenderness' (Jane Edwardes, *Time Out*) in her final instructions for the care of her children. Bosola had a more clearly redemptive role in this production than in most, and placed a shroud about her shoulders, sprinkled powder on her hair, and put a crucifix around her neck at the appropriate moments of his dirge (IV.ii.180, 189, 192). She knelt to death with great humility.

Some critics complained that the intensely realist acting made it difficult for this Duchess – who appeared innocent to a modern audience, and whose vengeful brothers acted outrageously – to be viewed as a tragic figure. Her death was pathetic, and deeply moving, but how could it be a tragedy if she had done nothing wrong? The play lacked 'a punishing fury' or 'moral urgency' (Nicholas de Jongh, *Guardian*).

The virtues of the production included the deep engagement of the audience with the Duchess, and the 'solicitous calm' (Charles Spencer, *Daily Telegraph*) with which Bosola assisted her in the *ars moriendi*, the art of dying well within the Church. In addition, despite the absence of the pervasive atmosphere of decadence of a Philip Prowse production, Bill Alexander had rescued the play from melodrama. In addition, one or two critics discovered a welcome feminist perspective: Ferdinand and the Cardinal express 'intense revulsion at the idea of a woman freely choosing according to her sexual desire' (Jane Edwardes, *Time Out*); and 'the Duchess offends against male power and its supportive hierarchy' (Jim Hiley, *Listener*).

Even though neither of the Bosolas (different actors at each theatre) seems to have plumbed the moral dilemma that is central to the character – 'That we cannot be suffered / To do good when we have a mind to it!' (IV.ii.389–9) – they were both effectively sinister, and established a good rapport with the audience. Ferdinand was praised for being played 'not as a howling lunatic, but as a haunted guilt-ridden creature' (Michael Billington, *Guardian*), but the realist style of the production gave the actor an insuperable problem with making Ferdinand's Act V lycanthropia avoid parody. He was strongly supported, though, by a fat, repellent, and sadistic Cardinal. By the time the production got to the Pit, there was no longer audience laughter at the final deaths; the influence of the Duchess's death was holding the play, as it should.

Overall, this was a production more in the tradition of Peggy Ashcroft's warmly human portrayals than of the ritualistic formalism of Philip Prowse's concepts. It went beyond the Ashcroft approach, however, in the detailed intelligence of the playing, in the ambition of interpreting the entire play uncut (at least in Stratford), and in a rare attempt to present a providentialist reading of Acts IV and V (see pp. 135–6). And it did this in the intimate environments of two small theatres with audience on three sides, both theatres more akin to the indoor 'private' theatre for which *The Duchess of Malfi* seems to have been originally written (see pp. 2–4), than for the large proscenium-arch theatres that were more common for twentieth-century professional productions.

Modernist rethinking: Cheek by Jowl, 1995

Cheek by Jowl was by 1995 fifteen years old, and the company had established a significant reputation for uncluttered staging and a fresh look at the classics. Director Declan Donnellan described the company at the time as 'picture restorers, stripping away the veneer of sentimental varnish that plays have accrued over the years' (Nightingale).

Their *The Duchess of Malfi* in 1995–96 had the sparest of sets: dark green curtains swagged back, chess-board squares painted on the floor, and the odd handsome chair or table. In part such simplicity was a function of this being a touring production. After opening in England in mid September 1995 they were off to Rome, Dublin, Melbourne, Bucharest, and New York (with weeks in Oxford and Blackpool squeezed in) before they opened at Wyndham's Theatre in London in late December. The company's policy was to continue rehearsing and altering plays on tour, so any description tends to be a snapshot of performance at a particular time and place.

The chess-board image of the stage was clearly a metaphor for the rigid rules governing princes of church and state; this was emphasized by the highly choreographed opening, with the entire court onstage in a frozen tableau, then each character turning ninety degrees before first speaking. Bosola, after being suborned by Ferdinand (with the Duchess sitting onstage at the time, though not part of the action), directed his sententious rhyming exit couplet (I.i.289–90) to the audience, a technique that caught the way these *sententiae* work structurally, slightly apart from the rest of the play (see pp. 13–14). And then he stood stock still. Into the silence that followed Delio injected two of his lines from Act III: 'In such a deformed silence, witches whisper / Their charms' (III.iii.58–9). At the word 'whisper', the courtiers, who were onstage through much of the play as a kind of chorus, started muttering, thus reinforcing a sense of self-referential theatricalism:

> This sort of thing, like wearing masks or having characters who should be off-stage standing on one side beadily observing the action [which the Duchess did throughout Act V], is part of the modernist theatrical vocabulary of the theatre. ... what you are about to see is not life but an artefact, not reality but a play that they are about to perform.
>
> (John Peter, *Sunday Times*)

One might have expected the reference to 'witches...charms' to serve as a pointed introduction to the entry of the Cardinal with the Duchess so that the two brothers could catechize their sister, but the text of the play was so cut and rearranged that in fact the lines were followed by Antonio and Delio's description of the 'three fair medals' (I.i.188) from more than a hundred lines earlier in the play. During this sequence each of the three in turn was being dressed by attendants for a formal occasion: 'he should have been Pope' (163) said Antonio as the Cardinal was robed in his richest ecclesiastical attire. Ferdinand was dressed in Edwardian court dress, his black tunic adorned with gold epaulettes, a plume in his elaborate hat. The young blonde Duchess wore a floor-length dress, and was topped off with a tiara like royalty. Each came into focus as Antonio commented on them. Antonio himself was in wing collar, black frock coat, and pinstripe trousers, while Bosola's black shirt, breeches, and high boots, and the courtiers entirely in black, invoked the power structure of Mussolini's fascist Italy of the 1920s and 30s.

Once the Duchess and her brothers were formally attired, they and the entire court formed a religious procession with church acolytes singing a doxology, the stage bathed in golden light. 'The omnipresence of black-suited figures doubling as *Gloria*-chanting acolytes and sinister fascist henchmen conjures up a world in which religious and political power conceals worm-eaten corruption' (Michael Billington, *Country Life*).

The 'worm-eaten corruption' was evident not just from Bosola's first dealings with the Cardinal, and Ferdinand's bribery of him, but also from the way in which the formal grandeur of the court was disrupted by the Duchess and her brothers abruptly breaking decorum by laughing wildly, shedding their royal robes and headgear, urgently reaching for whisky and cigarettes. They displayed the intimate knowledge of each other that signalled growing up together: the Duchess kissed the Cardinal, he clouted Ferdinand as he left, and she gave Ferdinand a petulant slap as soon as the Cardinal had gone. Then she allowed what started as a jokey nursery hug from her twin to become more sensual than sisterly. Clearly both his siblings knew that Ferdinand needed to be kept under control, and the Duchess appeared to be slightly complicit in humouring his ambiguous sexuality. A moment later he lunged at her with their 'father's poniard' (331), again in a jokey manner, but followed by a freeze that gave the image worrying force. Far from being a picture of happy families, the presentation suggested to many critics a dysfunctional royal family – the real house of Windsor was seldom out of the British press and the public mind in the mid nineties, not long before the death of Princess Diana.

The production deliberately rejected the concept of the Duchess as a victim, a portrayal that had been consistent from the nineteenth century and through the twentieth, whether in the dignified transcendence of a Peggy Ashcroft or the overwhelming visual imagery of a Philip Prowse. Indeed, the early eyewitness evidence suggests, as does the text to most readers, that the play has always shown the Duchess in that light (see p. 3). But a modernist approach is based on a deliberate rejection of traditional interpretations and of any accepted set of critical assumptions. Neither text nor subtext is sacred.

The Duchess, Anastasia Hille, refused to appear a victim. She was of the powerful elite, but damaged by it too, brittle and neurotic, autocratic and unpredictable. As she wooed Antonio she vamped him in the manner of a woman used to getting what she wanted, and she wasted no time. But she also retrieved her ring. She was in control. The erotic charge of her stepping out of her golden sheath dress almost naked was quickly undercut by her donning a dress padded to represent her pregnancy in II.i. The relationship with Antonio rapidly deteriorated. His powerlessness led him to petulance and the bottle, whereas she swung moment to moment between arrogance, desire, and sardonic laughter at herself. Most critics saw her as trapped in her public persona, but desperately trying to discover who she really was. Donnellan's view of the play was that 'love is completely removed, almost as if a colour has been sucked out of the spectrum' (Nightingale).

When the neurotic Ferdinand invaded her chamber in III.ii, Hille could not have been further from the usual interpretation. At 'I pray sir, hear me: I am married' (III.ii.82) she caught her brother off guard, slapped him down to the floor, jumped on him, and threatened him with his own knife before laughing, pouring herself a whisky, and returning to examine her hair again. As he stormed about she gave a 'wanker' gesture, mocked his words, and refused to take him seriously. Then her mood switched again, and she briefly cuddled and comforted him prior to his exit. (Not taking Ferdinand seriously, not being frightened of him, would in most productions make her scheme for Antonio's escape appear utterly arbitrary and unmotivated; in this production so much was arbitrary that one searched for explanation in the Duchess's mood swings and neuroses. Perhaps her apparent nonchalance was assumed, relying on force of will alone? Perhaps emotionally she was either afraid, or secretly welcoming the approaching disaster that would reveal her real self?)

When arrest and imprisonment came, she again seemed to refuse to take them seriously. She angrily objected to Ferdinand subjecting her to a game of blind man's buff in IV.i with the dead hand; she screamed when she finally realized (long after the audience) what she was holding, and dropped it; but a few moments later she picked it up and dropped it in a wastebasket as if this was the sort of prank Ferdinand had played all his life. She did not admit the threat, and paid little attention to the effigies of her dead husband and children. Even in IV.ii she kicked over the cross the very religious Cariola was praying at, and accepted the gift of a toy crown from the Madmen with ironic self-mockery. Whereas 'I am Duchess of Malfi still' (IV.ii.141) was for Peggy Ashcroft a proud assertion of integrity, for Hille it meant, according to Donnellan, 'Oh God, I'm the bloody Duchess of Malfi *still*' (Nightingale). Only gradually did her ironic sense of the absurdity of her situation lead her to 'humility … through neurotic despair' (Michael Billington, *Country Life*). She had shed her aristocratic persona, but it was far from clear what she found underneath. 'She may be psychologically fascinating but she is also, curiously, emotionally unenthralling' (James Christopher, *Time Out*).

Ferdinand was portrayed as what more than one critic called a 'damaged child', with the giggles, tantrums, and sexuality of the nursery. His hysteria and sudden mood changes could usually be controlled by his siblings, but his weakness of personality, combined with Renaissance power, made him terrifyingly dangerous. His infantile love for his sister generated emotions he neither understood nor controlled. Whereas the Cardinal's icy sadism was clearly evil, Ferdinand was hardly rational.

Just as the three royal figures were interpreted as a mass of contradictions, the production resisted single established meanings for words, or visual coherence with speech. Early in the apricot scene, when the Duchess asked Antonio about the French courtiers keeping their hats on even 'in the presence', and urged him to 'Put on your hat' (II.i.124, 129), both the public discussion of protocol before royalty, and the secret messages she conveyed to Antonio, were absurd because none of the courtiers had hats. In the same scene, Bosola comments about 'How greedily she eats them!' (151), but the Duchess had in this production already thrown away her half-eaten apricot at one of her courtiers. When Julia wooed Bosola, despite her language ('now I woo you') she first shot at him and then on 'I am sudden' (V.ii.192) anally raped him with her pistol. She seemed to be taking her revenge on the Cardinal (who sadistically twisted her nipple earlier in the play), and perhaps all men, rather than doing anything that seems expressed in the language of the play. Like the rearrangement of lines and bits of scenes, it forced one to look at the play anew, but also forced acceptance or rejection of what seemed, to any traditional critic, an arbitrary forcing of new meaning against the grain of the text.

The principal victim of the interpretation seems to have been Bosola. Whereas a strong Bosola can usually save even a mediocre production, and very few productions can succeed with a weak Bosola, here Bosola was hardly needed. He was played (not for the first time) as a Scot, an outsider among the English accents, and 'less a despairing malcontent than a grim mercenary' (Nicholas de Jongh, *Evening Standard*). With his lines severely cut, especially those in which the character establishes a jovial but sardonic complicity with the audience, and including his long final speech of explanation of his motives (which could hardly apply in this production), the actor could not be held wholly responsible for appearing weak and uninteresting.

At the end of the play the entire cast came to life again, but in a frozen tableau as at the opening, and with the principal characters posed as if for a family photo. The play was thus bookmarked by the two tableaux, with of course an implication of the ending already inevitable from the beginning.

Overall, critics were almost unanimous in recognizing the intelligence, craft, and interest of the production, but were divided on whether the gains matched the losses. For some, the director had thwarted the playwright:

> There's no wrenching horror or demoralization – rather a tremulous defiance. ... Websterian extremity is missing.
>
> (Nicholas de Jongh, *Evening Standard*)

No one could deny that it is powerfully conceived, lucid and sexy. But in this brittle, glamorous world, Webster's tragedy emerges as something cool, artful and slow. ... This production catches its own reflection.

(Robert Butler, *Independent on Sunday*)

For others, Cheek by Jowl had shed a new light on the play:

Donnellan ... builds up a picture of a morally corrupt world in which political and religious absolutism goes hand in hand with sexual cruelty.

(Michael Billington, *Country Life*)

There is ... no mistaking the clarity and the claustrophobic power of the production, which chillingly captures a moral wasteland of the human soul.

(Charles Spencer, *Daily Telegraph*)

The director had heeded Webster's use of varied stage images to alert the audience to narrative development. A silent reading of its text can give little idea of the succession of events that are called into being. As these follow each other, a slowly maturing sense is given that these characters are striving restlessly to reach an end that was predicated long before they could have foreseen it. ... The large demands made on the actors' physical resources also contributed to the sense of a story moving ruthlessly – the actors seldom made it easy for each other – until everyone is played out. Perhaps Webster planned something like this, because [by the last act] exhausted and now only briefly assertive, the actors present their characters stumbling toward disintegration and the audience watches spellbound, even by the mere spectacle.

(Brown, 'Techniques of Restoration', p. 331)

5   The Play on Screen

The Duchess of Malfi was first broadcast on television by the BBC as early as 1938, the same year they presented the first Shakespeare play ever broadcast. BBC produced the play again 1949, as did the CBC in Canada in 1962, and French television in 1965. However, only one full television production and one filmed stage version are generally available, and they will be discussed here. There have been no feature films, although there have been both film and television adaptations; and many short appropriations can be found on YouTube.

On 10 October 1972, several years prior to the BBC/Time Life broadcasts and recordings of all of Shakespeare's plays, initially produced by Cedric Messina, *The Duchess of Malfi* was broadcast in Britain. It was produced by Messina for the BBC, and directed by James McTaggart. And when it was also broadcast on the American PBS network (slightly cut) in 1975, and widely elsewhere around the world, Webster's play reached a wider audience than all the stage productions since 1614 put together.

The made-for-TV film was, unusually, done as an 'outside broadcast' rather than in a studio. It is set in a real Jacobean manor, Chastleton House in the Cotswolds, and thus places the action in a more domestic court than one usually sees on stage, but a court that is complete and entirely believable. Differences in social rank are emphasized by the Jacobean costuming (Bosola in leather like a soldier, for instance, unlike the other men); and the extent to which the Duchess is flouting social convention in her wooing of Antonio is equally clearly portrayed in the acting. Eileen Atkins as the Duchess always retains the arrogance that makes her her brothers' sister, but also makes her vulnerability and warmth very moving in her wooing of Antonio. The camera keeps Michael Bryant's straightforward, if slightly dull Bosola well to the fore also, particularly in the Duchess's death scene (IV.ii), so that the notorious problem of maintaining interest in Act V is largely overcome by the attention that has been visually directed to him. The Ferdinand of Charles Kay is not so much underplayed as played very quietly; his ever-shifting eyes suggest incipient derangement right from the start, but the more grotesque bits of his madness are cut. The acting of the rest of the cast is similarly subdued to fit the small screen in a realistic mode. Soliloquies and asides are often done as more psychologically persuasive interior monologues using a voice-over technique.

Realism, of course, is the dominant mode in film and television drama. As one might expect, the more formal elements of the play are largely cut: Bosola's scenes with the Old Lady in II.i and II.ii; most of Julia's first scene with the Cardinal, and all of Delio's attempt to bribe her in that scene; the tale of the Salmon in III.v (though the Reputation fable is retained in III.ii); the madmen's song and Bosola's dirge in IV.ii; and all of V.i, and considerable sections of the rest of Act V. The story is made believable at a human level, and emotion and coherence of character are to the fore; what is perhaps put at risk, or at least not emphasized, is the wider moral perspective of the tragedy.

However, the production occasionally moves into a more stylized mode that responds to Webster's emblematic theatrical patterning. When Bosola kills Antonio, not only is a twisting stairway a convincingly obscure space to explain the mistake in identification, but also a visual metaphor for the contorted labyrinth into which Bosola's confused ethics and actions have brought him.

The stairway also appears to serve as an emblem of Fortune. Antonio is on a stairway in I.i as he sings the praises of the Duchess to Delio (a scene, incidentally, that has lost the stage iconography written in by Webster, in which the two brothers and their sister Duchess are present on stage as Antonio and Delio comment). Antonio is overlooked by a dark family portrait as he thinks of the Duchess, then is met 'between floors', neither up nor down, by Cariola, who sends him to an assignation higher in the house, indeed to dangerous heights he had not aspired to. These are the same stairs on which we constantly discover Bosola hovering between two worlds, where *he* has *his* assignation with the ambiguous figure of Julia: and down which he descends to murder Antonio in error.

In contrast, the Duchess and her attendants are discovered at I.i.292 walking in the open and extensive grounds outside the house as Ferdinand and the Cardinal catechize her about remarriage. But the straight paths, regimented hedges, and the stern symmetry of the house facade, remind us very clearly of the position of the Duchess in a society with codes of conduct as highly structured and constraining as their elaborate court garments. The action is similarly rigid, for the courtiers retain their symmetrically spaced stations at a determined distance behind the Duchess and her two brothers, and halt or advance in strict synchronization with her pace. The amplified sound of feet on the gravelled path leads to a startling silence when they stop. Concealment is an impossibility in so public a society.

The formality of setting and action is further emphasized by purely cinematic means. Sound is subtly orchestrated. The composition of the shot is formal and symmetrical, absolutely front-on. The three principal actors are centred, the attendants framed between and behind them, with the house four-square in the background. Camera movement is a direct track back, retaining the symmetry and contrasting sharply with the fluid camera movement used up to this point of the film. Finally, the sequence is one long take lasting one minute forty seconds. The traditional shot and reverse shot technique that we are used to as a film convention of realistic dialogue (as in the wooing scene between the Duchess and Antonio) has been eschewed in favour of a deliberate formalism of every aspect of the shot.

Although the dominant mode is realism, therefore, the film also responds on occasion to the self-conscious theatricalism with which Webster patterns his language and action.

In contrast to the BBC's television film on location, the Stage on Screen company performed the play at the Greenwich Theatre in London (directed by Elizabeth Freestone) specifically to be filmed as an educational DVD. There is no attempt to present Webster's drama within a real historical context; here, the reality is the performance of the play onstage in front of an audience. The stage design is abstract: a black and white chequerboard floor surrounded on three sides by a black wall with doors. Usually the central area only is lit, so that the performance seems uneasily isolated in space, and surrounded by blackness, or by dim lighting from offstage allowing only the outline of open doors to be made out through drifting smoke. The stage is nearly always bare, with only occasional large properties used (a chaise longue and a cheval glass for the Duchess's chamber in III.ii; an altar for the shrine at Loretto; the waxworks in IV.i at one of the upper windows). Costume appears modernish, tending to reference 1930s fascist Italy, but clearly generic and generalized (e.g., a long black leather coat for Bosola, a red sash to designate Duke Ferdinand).

The deliberate theatricalism in design is matched by the staging. Characters are normally alone on an absolutely bare stage, and often stand much farther apart than we would expect. Movement is limited also, both for speakers and listeners. This avoidance of the techniques of stage realism creates a sense of formality that is almost mannerist in style. It also throws attention strongly on to the language of the play, and the text is almost uncut.

The production opens with an invented dumb show in which all the characters enter in minimum light and form a tableau of mourning (presumably for the Duchess's dead husband) as an artillery salute is heard in the distance. The red robes of the Cardinal (Mark Hadfield) provide the only colour among the unrelieved black of everyone else, but the Duke (Tim Steed) twitches his face briefly, attracting attention. Then the play proper starts, with a prolix Antonio (a fascinating performance by Edmund Kingsley) and Delio commenting on most of the court business from one of the upper windows, retaining that sense of observation that is notably missing from the BBC version. The Duchess (Aislin McGuckin) is aggressively willing to deceive her brothers (with none of the BBC ambiguity about whether she is interrupted after "I'll never marry" [I.i.302]), and her wooing of Antonio is more brisk, intellectual, and amused at his fear than emotionally loving.

Tim Treloar as Bosola gives perhaps the most interesting performance of all, as a malcontent whose satiric energy is angry rather than melancholic. Unlike the often unreadable BBC Bosola, and many stage Bosolas, Treloar's demonstrates a credible honesty rather than dissimulation in praising the 'dismissed' Antonio at III.ii.230–76 (reinforced by delivering 279–82 direct to the audience), a savage desire to help the Duchess from the moment of her exit in IV.i, and an unswerving commitment to Antonio and the memory of the Duchess for the rest of the play. As a result, his lines of self-loathing (e.g., IV.ii.322–74) carry the ring of truth.

Comparison of this production with the BBC version is instructive, and both have their strengths. Whereas the constricting BBC period costumes imply the codes and hierarchies of the Renaissance, the relaxed modern garb used by Stage on Screen throws more weight on individual personality (especially evident in the very divergent approaches to the Duchess's wooing of Antonio). Julia enters with the Duchess rather than with Castruchio (so BBC) in I.i.

In Act II the retention by Stage on Screen of Bosola's malcontent satire on Castruchio and the Old Woman, and his own 'meditation' in II.i (all cut by the BBC) builds his presence and importance in a way that provides an additional context to the apricots episode later in the scene. And throughout the performance Bosola plays many of his lines straight to the audience, as no doubt Webster expected. In II.v Ferdinand's violent 'palsy' (55) compared to the Cardinal's phlegmatic calm is better caught in the BBC version, and the Stage on Screen Ferdinand, thinking of his sister sexually, starts to masturbate with his hand in his trouser pocket, which seems both more crass and less ambiguous than what Webster has written.

Stage and Screen opens Act III with the sounds of troops marching, and a striking shift of many characters into uniform, thus preparing the ground for III.iii. In III.ii the BBC establishes more love and emotion between the Duchess and Antonio (and Cariola), and uses film composition to emphasize the bed in conjunction with Ferdinand's stealthy entry into his sister's chamber, whereas Stage on Screen places more emphasis on the dagger, and the Duchess's brave reaction to the threat of death. Each interpretation can serve the play well in different ways, but bringing Antonio on at 87 and then forcing him offstage backwards, so Ferdinand won't see him after all, seems unfortunately comedic. Stage and Screen, despite its insistence on Ferdinand's incestuous feelings for the Duchess, also changes 'thy husband's bones' (113) to 'our father's bones', thereby shifting the emphasis away from remarriage, and Ferdinand's possibly unconscious substitution of himself for her late husband, to family honour (presumably to match 'my father's poniard' at I.i.331). For the arming of the Cardinal in III.iv, Stage on Screen provides soldiers (rather than Q1's 'Churchmen') to sing an eerie version of the 'ditty' that 'The author disclaims...to be his' (7.9–11), whereas BBC relies on more mundane ecclesiastical organ music.

Although Stage on Screen keeps the lighting very low while Ferdinand is presenting the dead man's hand to the Duchess in IV.i, the staging allows the audience to see the deceit before she does (unlike the BBC), and therefore to concentrate on her reaction. The Duchess's rage and anguish are strongly played, but unlike the BBC

version, the waxworks are distant (at an upper level) and theatrically
lit so as to appear abstract, without much threat or horror. Bosola,
however, is appalled at the trick played on the Duchess. His anger and
revulsion at his role as the Duchess's executioner carries into IV.ii;
and despite the absence of the coffin as a 'present' and her 'last presence chamber' (165, 170; see BBC), the death scene is powerful, and
pushes Bosola into his determination to revenge her.

The final act, so heavily cut by the BBC, is relatively uncut by Stage
on Screen, thus getting the benefit of the continuing importance of
Delio. V.ii carries little of the mad threat of the Duke, and the Julia–
Bosola scene is a bit perfunctory, but the difficult action around the
death of Antonio is well managed, Bosola's anguish strongly played,
and Antonio and the Duchess's young son inscrutably surveys the
carnage as Delio delivers the concluding speech about '*integrity of life*'
(V.v.120). As the actors rise from death to take their curtain call, and
then leave, all that is left is a bright red pool of blood in the centre of
the black and white stage.

'A fast-food McMalfi'

Mike Figgis's film *Hotel* is less a film of *The Duchess of Malfi* than a
bizarre soft-porn exploration of it. Pascale Aebischer describes the
plot, 'which includes Jacobean excesses such as cannibalism, murder,
usurpation, necrophilia, and revenge', as 'self-reflexively [centring]
on an international film crew following the rules set down in the
Dogme95 manifesto of filmmaking to produce what Figgis has called
a 'sort of "period punk" adaptation' of the play as a 'metacinematic
reflection' (Aebischer, 'Shakespearean Heritage', p. 280). The script-
writer who has adapted Webster explains at one point that they have
often 'cut the iambic pentameters, heptameters, archaisms in order
to create a fast-food McMalfi'. This playful deconstruction occasionally provides a recognizable moment of the original play, as when
the actors playing the Duchess and Antonio are found practising
the wooing scene in traditional mode (very similar, in fact, to that
of the BBC version). The director listens a moment, then sarcastically supports them trying the scene 'all different ways, and I love
the Merchant-Ivory version you're doing at the moment. Sweet,
pungent smell of rose meadows, Earl Grey. ... That sort of thing. It's

fucking shit!' Far from wanting a heritage film with flowers and scented English tea, the director wants Antonio to imagine himself in mean streets, to force the Duchess against a wall and 'fuck her like a criminal!' (Aebischer, 'Shakespearean Heritage', p. 295). The eventual scene is even more extreme: as she delivers the Webster lines from the wooing scene the Duchess sodomizes Antonio, and at her climax gives birth to two obviously plastic babies while embracing Antonio and kissing Cariola. It is difficult to know whether this is a highly theorized deconstruction of the transgression of social and sexual boundaries of which the Duchess is accused, or is simply a voyeuristic and deliberately deviant assault on mainstream culture.

6   Critical Assessments

Early criticism

The enthusiasm of Webster's fellow playwrights for *The Duchess of Malfi* (see p. 3) was already being qualified by the mid seventeenth century when Abraham Wright complained, with reference to the time elapsed between Acts II and III, that 'against all the laws of the scene, the business was two years a-doing' (Moore, p. 35). Wright is referring to the neoclassical rule of the unity of time, just as the eighteenth-century playwright Lewis Theobald did when he adapted the play as *The Fatal Secret* (1733). He described Webster as having 'a strong and impetuous genius, but withal a most wild and indigested one. ... As for rules, he either knew them not, or thought them too servile a restraint. Hence it is that he skips over years. ...' (Preface).

In the nineteenth century Romantic criticism replaced neoclassical rules; moments of sublimity were more valued than regularity. In 1808 Charles Lamb initiated an admiring critical view of *The Duchess of Malfi* thus:

> To move horror skillfully, to touch a soul to the quick, to lay upon fear as much as it can bear, to wean and weary a life till it is ready to drop, and then step in with mortal instruments to take its last forfeit – this only a Webster can do. Writers of an inferior genius may 'upon horror's head horrors accumulate', but they cannot do this. They mistake quantity for quality, they 'terrify babes with painted devils', but they know not how a soul is capable of being moved; their terrors want dignity, their affrightments are without decorum.

(Moore, p. 52)

Increasingly Webster was also acknowledged as a dramatic poet capable of sublime poetry, suiting the Romantic enthusiasm for plucking poetic excerpts into bouquets. William Hazlitt in 1819 exemplifies the Romantic response to moments of powerful emotion in the play:

> ... her last word, 'Mercy', which she recovers just enough strength enough to pronounce; her proud answer to her tormentors, who taunt her with her degradation and misery – 'But [*sic*] I am Duchess of Malfy still' – as if the heart rose up, like a serpent coiled, to resent the indignities put upon it, and being struck at, struck again; and the staggering reflection her brother makes on her death, 'Cover her face: my [*sic*] eyes dazzle: she died young!'
>
> (Moore, p. 62)

But many critics would also complain that Webster did not sustain this level for the entirety of his plays. John Wilson, for instance (writing as 'H. M.' in *Blackwood's Magazine* in 1818), says that '[s]ome single scenes are to be found in his works inferior in power of passion to nothing in the whole range of the drama. ... But our sympathies, suddenly awakened, are allowed as suddenly to subside' (Moore, p. 56).

A more serious accusation was that Webster's playwriting skills were limited to melodrama and horror. George Henry Lewes, reviewing the first major nineteenth-century production of the play (see p. 105) in 1850, thought that '[i]nstead of "holding the mirror up to nature", this drama holds the mirror up to Madame Tussaud's, and emulates her "chamber of horrors" but the "worst remains behind", and this is the motiveless and false exhibition of human nature' (Moore, p. 86). This is a two-pronged attack on Webster's work as (a) exhibiting horror for its own sake, just like Madame Tussaud's famous museum of grisly waxworks, and (b) failing to write realistic characters with adequate motivation. And it inspired George Bernard Shaw's later condemnation of Webster as 'the Tussaud laureate'.

Widely divergent opinions on Webster's qualities became the norm. In the 1880s the poet Algernon Swinburne was in the vanguard of defenders:

> Mere literary power, mere poetic beauty, mere charm of passionate or pathetic fancy, we find in varying degrees dispersed among [all the other Elizabethan and Jacobean playwrights]; but the crowning gift of imagination, the power to make us realize that thus and not otherwise it was,

that thus and not otherwise it must have been, was given – except by exceptional fits and starts – to none of the poets of their time but only to Shakespeare and to Webster.

(Moore, p. 111)

The late nineteenth century, however, was increasingly moving towards 'realism' as the governing mode of dramatic writing and theatrical presentation. William Archer, the great champion of Henrik Ibsen as a realist dramatist, was understandably antagonistic to 'the Lamb tradition' of praise:

When we find a playwright, in his two acknowledged masterpieces, drenching the stage with blood even beyond the wont of his contemporaries and searching out every possible circumstance of horror – ghosts, maniacs, severed limbs and all the paraphernalia of the charnel-house and the tomb – with no conceivable purpose except just to make our flesh creep, may we not reasonably, or rather must we not inevitably, conclude that he either reveled in 'violent delights' for their own sake, or wantonly pandered to the popular craving for them? ... Webster was not, in the special sense of the word, a great dramatist, but was a great poet who wrote haphazard dramatic or melodramatic romances for an eagerly receptive but semi-barbarous public.

(Moore, 139–43)

This somewhat simple assessment was to recur for the next hundred years, including a late appearance in the film *Shakespeare in Love*.

Twentieth-century criticism

Attacks on Webster's right to be regarded as a major dramatist continued during the first half of the twentieth century. Noteworthy were two essays in the journal *Scrutiny*, which championed analysis over the Lamb tradition of appreciation. W. A. Edwards attacks Webster in a 1933 essay for failure of characterization; then, having convicted the characters of being static and inconsistent, for Webster's failure to make his moral maxims and *sententiae* appropriate to them. Another *Scrutiny* critic, Ian Jack, repeats the charge, and adds to it, in 1949:

There is no correspondence between the axioms and the life represented in the drama. This dissociation is the fundamental flaw in Webster. ... [He

has] no profound hold on any system of moral values. ... Webster, that is to
say, is a decadent.

(Hunter, pp. 159–64)

L. G. Salingar in 1956 is the last in the line of broad-brush condem-
nations, repeating Jack's verdict: 'Webster is sophisticated, but his
sophistication belongs to decadence'. Despite the poignancy of the
Duchess' death and a few other scenes, the 'remainder of the action
consists of tedious moralizing, posturing, and blood-and-thunder'
(pp. 349–52).

Appreciation was not entirely missing in this period, however.
A major stage revival in 1945 initiated a re-evaluation of the play
in the theatre (see pp. 105–7). And the popular detective novelist
Agatha Christie evidently saw that production, to judge by *Sleeping
Murder* (written in the 1940s, though not published until 1976), which
features the powerful theatrical experience of the play as the thematic
underpinning of her whole novel.

Webster's dramatic language

While T. S. Eliot had earlier referred to Webster and other Jacobean
writers as representing 'an artistic decline inevitable after the greatness of Shakespeare', he insisted that he did not wish

> to leave you with the suspicion that his work shows also a *moral* deca-
> dence. In a world without meaning there can ... be horror, but not trag-
> edy. Webster's drama is tragic, and belongs in a world in which right and
> wrong, the soul and its destiny, are still important things.

(Rabkin, p. 102)

As early as 1924 Eliot deplored the tendency since Lamb for critics
on both sides of the fence (he cites Swinburne and Archer) to accept
implicitly a distinction between literature and drama. Eliot argues
instead that the problem lies in our failure to recognize that the 'aim
of the Elizabethans was to attain complete realism without surren-
dering any of the advantages which as artists they observed in unreal-
istic conventions' (Eliot, p. 116). Given Eliot's commitment to poetry,
his attention to Webster's language was illuminating: the dramatic
complexity, irony, and mordant wit of the writing reminded him of
the metaphysical poet John Donne.

Understanding of Webster's style was further developed by Hereward T. Price in an article that stressed the interplay of the literary and dramatic force of the language. Webster 'gives us figure in action and figure in language' (Hunter, p. 178), an intimate correspondence of the performed action and the poetic linguistic impulse:

> Figure-in-action and figure-in-word reinforce one another. [Webster] repeats his theme tirelessly, spinning innumerable variations with his figures of the magnificent outer show and the inner corruption, of life, fortune, hopes that look so fair and delude us utterly, of the many bitter, twisted ironies of the difference between appearance and reality.
>
> (Hunter, p. 201)

The debt to other authors in Webster's writing was catalogued in mid century by John Dent's *John Webster's Borrowings*, which reveals the unusual extent to which the dramatist draws his dialogue from his sources. As if constructing a detailed mosaic, Webster will meticulously adjust, reshape, improve, and insert his borrowings from a huge range of authors he has read. Such use of other writers' materials was common-place at the time (complimentary imitation, though now it would be regarded as plagiarism), but seldom did it result in such a dense, polished, and sententious style as is now recognized as characteristically Websterian.

Another study of Webster's writing habits concentrated on his use of his sources. Gunnar Boklund in 1962 notes, for instance, that whereas Painter's *Palace of Pleasure* (see pp. 95–104) is harshly critical of the Duchess for both her lust and her lack of social decorum in marrying Antonio, Webster's heroine is merely headstrong; and that Webster increases the villainy of the Cardinal and Ferdinand. The cumulative results of these and many other changes to the source material is, in Boklund's view, a theme of almost 'unrelieved futility' (p. 130).

Themes and morality

C. V. Boyer in 1914 was the first critic to maintain that Webster had a clear moral vision, and the question of just how to interpret the themes of the plays started to take centre stage. Rupert Brooke's summation at the end of his 1916 book foreshadows elements of Boklund:

The world called Webster is a peculiar one. ... Human beings are writhing grubs in an immense night. And the night is without stars or moons. But it has sometimes a certain quietude in its darkness; but not very much.

(Brooke, pp. 161–2)

Una Ellis-Fermor in 1936 explained this pessimism in terms of the historical moment in which the Jacobean dramatists found themselves, the early seventeenth century in England being profoundly unsettled in religious, political, and social beliefs. Webster 'brings his people, by the most careful preparation, to the position in which, if ever, a man should see absolute reality – and before them is only a mist' (cited in Gunby, 'Critical Backstory', p. 24). Only the Duchess uncertainly recognizes it for what it is: a world without meaning or hope.

Lord David Cecil, however, perceived a harsh but coherent Calvinist world:

a fallen place in which suffering outweighs happiness, and all activities are tainted with sin. ... Yet it is also a place where the moral law cannot be thwarted indefinitely. ... Heaven is just, for all the apparent horror of man's life. In the end virtue is glorified; but only beyond death.

Cecil valuably notes in passing how attention to Bosola's sinfulness nullifies the frequent complaint about the early death of the Duchess rendering Act V anti-climactic:

Though [the Duchess] is the heroine in the sense that she is the chief object of our sympathies, she does not provide the chief motive force in the action; nor is it, in her relation to that action, that the theme of the play is to be found. This theme, as always with Webster, is the act of sin and its consequences.

(Hunter, pp. 150–54)

Robert Ornstein's *The Moral Vision of Jacobean Tragedy* (1960) takes a less religious approach to morality, praising the Duchess as the only character with 'the strength to endure – the cardinal and redeeming virtue in Webster's tragic universe' (p. 140). Nevertheless, he says, 'The Duchess' strength is not a lonely existential awareness of self but a remembrance of love. ... [She] is the only one to move out of self ... and upward in serene religious faith' (p. 148). John Russell

Brown's 1964 Revels edition is deeply sympathetic to the play, but more thoroughly existentialist in trying to explain the contested search for a unified moral vision. In a kind of portmanteau embrace of conflicting views, he says it is 'a unity of empirical, responsible, skeptical, unsurprised, and deeply perceptive concern for the characters and society portrayed' (p. xlix).

Elizabeth Brennan's New Mermaids edition appeared the same year as Brown's, but Brennan argues that Webster displays a traditional Christian world; moreover, one in which Bosola plays a profound role in assisting the Duchess to avoid the mortal sin of despair, and instead to '[r]emember that [she is] a Christian' (IV.i.74–5). Peter B. Murray's book on Webster similarly applies a Christian-Stoic point of view to the death of the Duchess, and D. C. Gunby carries this further:

> Webster uses this conflict to demonstrate that a man can be at once an agent of God and of the Devil. Bosola torments the Duchess yet comforts her, destroys yet saves her. In a conflict like this the Jacobeans firmly believed that God could always nullify the intrigues of the Devil.
>
> (Morris, p. 190)

Bettie Anne Doebler's 1980 study of the *ars moriendi* tradition – the art of dying well – adds further historical detail to a Christian interpretation of the play.

Style and meaning

A study of Webster's style has been productive as well, with Travis Bogard's *The Tragic Satire of John Webster* (1955) particularly influential. He argues that Webster's tragedy is achieved through a satiric vision of the world:

> The ultimate tragedy of Webster's world is not the death of any individual but the presence of evil and decay which drags all mankind to death. The function of the satire is to reveal man's common mortality and his involvement in evil; the tragic story is the story of a few who find courage to defy such revelation. ... Websterian tragedy is great because of its fusion of satire and tragedy.
>
> (Bogard, p. 147)

Bogard's attention to satire allowed Webster's *sententiae* a constructive role within a coherent dramaturgy. Subsequent critical studies of Webster in terms of genre have also been instructive. Ralph Berry in 1972 suggested that the mannered style of baroque art was the most useful lens through which to interpret the often intractable critical uncertainties about how to view Webster's work.

Jacqueline Pearson's *Tragedy and Tragicomedy in the Plays of John Webster* (1980) finds not only Bogard's satire, but also the generic attributes of tragicomedy, or at least parodic 'anti-tragedy':

> The fourth act of *The Duchess of Malfi*, then, presents a tragedy in which a good woman achieves a tragic self-assertion. This tragic centre, however, emerges from a mass of anti-tragic material: a masque which provides a grotesquely distorted view of the play itself, a parody of the tragic moment as Cariola refuses tragedy and Ferdinand perverts tragic catharsis, and a miniature tragicomedy as the Duchess briefly revives.…the focus shifts from tragedy to inversions and parodies of tragedy.…
>
> (Pearson, pp. 88–9)

Lee Bliss is similarly concerned with genre, suggesting that '[t]he last act's farcical treatment of tragic motifs is grotesquely compelling, unsatisfying, and beyond easy dismissal.…[s]etting *The Duchess of Malfi*'s affirmations against farce's closed world of ultimately meaningless aggression.…(pp. 169–70).

Structure

One of the most productive twentieth-century approaches to explaining how Webster wrote, and therefore how the play should be understood, was to replace nineteenth-century accusations of structural incompetence with closer and more sympathetic investigations. M. C. Bradbrook's *Themes and Conventions of Elizabethan Tragedy* was a major contribution. She points out how misleading an expectation of the 'realism' of a well-made-play is, both in character and structure.

Inga-Stina Ekeblad's 1958 article, 'The 'Impure Art' of John Webster', remains one of the most important contributions to detailed analysis of the conventions that Webster was working with. Why, she asks, does Webster introduce a rabble of singing madmen into IV.ii, the scene generally agreed to be the play's 'most penetrating piece of character analysis' (cited in Hunter, p. 204). Her answer, drawing on Eliot's comment about the 'impure art' of the Elizabethans, is that the grotesque madmen are in effect a masque, or more properly an anti-masque, within the framework of the Duchess's death scene, which is itself structured as if it were a court masque:

> The action of the scene is grasped only by seeing both the basic framework and the masque structure, and the progressive interaction of the two. It is this structural counterpointing of 'convention' and 'realism', this concentrated 'impurity' of art, that gives the scene its peculiar nature; indeed, it contains the meaning of the scene.
>
> (Hunter, p. 205)

Christina Luckyj in 1989 and David Gunby in 2004 have independently demonstrated a structural coherence based not on a linear plot line, but on a non-linear pattern of 'juxtapositions, parallels and repetition':

> Like Shakespeare, Webster is less concerned with developing a causally linked narrative than with exploring and emphasizing the different aspects of a central experience. Like Shakespeare, Webster uses repetitive form, de-emphasizing the play's linear progression for the advantage of reworking and expanding his basic material.
>
> (Luckyj, *Winter's Snake*, pp. xx, 1)

For instance, the 'wooing' of Bosola in Act V by Julia is a grimly parodic reminder of the Duchess and Antonio in Act I, and Delio's theatrically self-conscious greeting of Antonio at the start of Act III echoes the start of Act I, alerting us to the pattern of repetition. David Gunby examines further the theatrical time gaps between the acts, and also identifies a 'two-movement structure' that 'provides a sense of artistic unity and progression' that has been all too little recognized ('Strong Commanding Art', p. 219).

In a now often-cited article, Catherine Belsey suggests that the failure of modern critical modes attuned to psychological realism to explain the play can be remedied by a realization that

> *The Duchess of Malfi* ... is a play poised, formally as well as historically, between the emblematic tradition of the medieval stage and the increasing commitment to realism of the post-Restoration theater.
>
> (Bloom, p. 97)

Belsey describes the way both emblem books and medieval plays rely on interpretation of concepts or arguments rather than the reproduction of outward appearance, and applies this to Webster:

> [T]he audience is repeatedly invited by the realist surface to expect the unfolding of a situation or the interplay of specific characters, only to find that the actual constantly resolves into abstraction, the characters into figures in a pattern. The imagery, both visual and verbal, often functions in a way that is emblematic rather than realistic, arresting the movement of the plot and placing the emphasis on significance rather than experience. The effect is a play the presents an anatomy of the world rather than a replica of it.
>
> (Bloom, p. 99)

Michael Neill also sees the play in emblematic terms. He suggests that our reaction to the physical structures required on stage (the shrine at Loretto, the waxwork bodies, the ruins and grave in V.iii) will interact with concepts of memorialization, from the dedicatory verses before the printed text to the final couplet of the play: '*Integrity of life is fame's best friend, / Which nobly, beyond death, shall crown the end*'. Neill concludes that the play, and especially the often-misunderstood Act V, should be seen as 'a dramatized pageant of Fame, bringing its monumental theme to life in a richly enacted metaphor' (Neill, p. 329).

New schools of criticism

In the late twentieth-century, literary and dramatic criticism underwent a revolution in which new historical, ideological, theatrical, practical, and academic approaches substantially modified what had gone before. Dympna Callaghan provides an excellent extended survey of post-2000 criticism in 'The State of the Art' (in Luckyj, *Critical Guide*, pp. 66–86). In terms of Webster and *The Duchess of Malfi*, three of these new 'schools' are of special significance: Historicist/Materialist criticism, Feminist criticism, and Theatrical and Performance based criticism and practice.

Materialist criticism

Sometimes known as New Historicism (especially in the US) or Cultural Materialism (especially in Britain, where it tends to be

more Marxist in orientation), materialist criticism confronts the
older 'essentialist' critical view of artistic genius as universal: as
transcending the time and place of composition. Rather, materialist critics stress the material circumstances of the writer's life and
work, of writing, performing, and publishing, and the ideologies of
politics, economics, gender, and other material conditions. Often,
historical anecdote is used as a way of opening up a new sense of
historicity for the modern reader. In addition, the left-wing stance
of the critic is evident; much of the research is explicitly designed
to demonstrate subversive and anti-authoritarian elements within
the play.

For instance, Frank Whigham's pioneering New Historicist article
'Sexual and Social Mobility in *The Duchess of Malfi*' analyses Ferdinand
and his sister Duchess 'in the light of class strata', and 'their mobile
servants Antonio and Bosola as employees and self-conceived social
inferiors'.

> Most readings of *The Duchess of Malfi* apply two categories of analysis:
> psychological inquiry (what are Ferdinand's motives? how should
> we understand Bosola?) and moral evaluation (what is the status
> of the Duchess's marriage to Antonio? how does he measure up to
> it?). ... Correlations between incest and promiscuity, ascribed and achieved
> status, community and alienation can help us chart this sprawling yet
> impacted play by situating it more firmly in Jacobean culture [with its]
> friction between the dominant social order and the emergent pressures
> toward social change.
>
> (Callaghan, *New Casebooks*, p. 167)

As the vocabulary and stress on class and employment suggest,
the analysis of Ferdinand's incest, the Duchess's decision to marry
beneath her rank, Antonio's insecurity at rising higher than a steward,
and Bosola's resentful position between feudal service and capitalist
employment in early seventeenth century Europe represents a sharp
break from 'most readings' prior to Whigham's 1985 article.

Like Whigham, Mary Beth Rose accepts that a full understanding
of the play requires attention to 'Jacobean social processes' (Rose,
cited in Callaghan, *New Casebooks*, p. 124), and her emphasis is
centrally on class and 'the Protestant conception of marriage as a
heroic endeavour' (p. 128). But she resists Whigham's dismissal of the
importance of the Duchess's sexuality. In addition, she challenges

Belsey's contention that private life was of necessity subordinate to public life:

> it is the full recognition of the importance of private life, here claiming equal status with public concerns, that makes her tragic stature possible. ... the heroics of marriage is associated with the bourgeois recognition of merit in determining status, rather than the aristocratic reliance on birth. ...

> (Rose, pp. 129–31)

Rose's densely argued and theorized approach includes analysis of the social conditions that enable tragedy to be written, and she concludes that Webster's final choice of tragic mode is elegiac and reactionary rather than radical.

Wendy Wall deploys a study of the 'syrup' that the Duchess urges Cariola to give her little boy 'for his cold' (IV.ii.203) to interrogate not only Rose's argument, but many of the materialist conclusions about 'affect' (emotion, feelings) as 'instrumental in ushering in a conceptual schema of separate private and public spheres' (Wall, p. 150). She offers a useful survey of how Belsey, Jardine, Jankowski, and several other recent critics have interpreted the importance of the domestic and private, and then offers her own contrary view:

> To state it crudely, critics discover proof, in the fourth act of this play, of a maternalism that is historically and generically novel albeit contested, and they rely on a standard historical narrative about domesticity's role in forging a new conception of privacy to frame their interpretations of motherhood and family.

> (Wall, p. 155)

Wall's close study of syrups as both medicine and 'sweetmeats' (candy; I.i.466), and their preparation sometimes including ingredients as mortal as ground human skulls, opens up an area of surprising complexity.

Callaghan's 'State of the Art' discusses a number of other materialist and historicist contributions to the debate. Her section headings alone – including Dead Bodies, Theatre and Performance, Religion, Sovereignty, and Wolves, Madness, etc. – give some sense of how varied that critical discourse now is. The most extensive, however, is Gender and Sexuality.

Feminist criticism

> The most crucial force shaping criticism on the play through the eighties
> and nineties was unquestionably feminism, which, rather than seeing the
> absence of a male protagonist as constituting nothing short of a funda-
> mental structural flaw, valued Webster's feminocentric vision. Feminist
> critics tended to see Webster as sympathetic towards women rather than
> as a misogynist playwright who presented his female characters like
> daughters of Eve who got what they deserved. ... [However, I] argued that
> feminist criticism did a disservice to Webster's remarkable Duchess by
> trying to press her into a female version of a male paradigm, a kind of 'great
> man' in drag.
>
> (Callaghan, 'State of the Art', p. 67)

Callaghan was and is herself a leading figure in this movement,
particularly with her 1989 book *Woman and Gender in Renaissance
Tragedy*. She also edited the 'New Casebooks' collection of largely
feminist essays from the 1980s and 1990s.

That collection includes an essay by Christy Desmet ('"Neither
Maid, Widow, nor Wife": Rhetoric of the Woman Controversy in
The Duchess of Malfi') now regarded as a classic of feminist criticism,
in which she argues that the sophisticated classically derived (and
male-oriented) rhetoric of the time is skilfully deployed to define
and subjugate the Duchess as, by definition, powerless because
female. Other essays include Karin S. Coddon on madness, Theodora
Jankowski's consideration of the slippery distinctions between the
female body politic and body natural, and Susan Wells on the nature
of representation.

Callaghan's wariness about over-simple feminist approbation for
the Duchess had already been aired by the remarkable Lisa Jardine.
Jardine warns against our being 'seduced' into accepting the 'force-
fulness and spirited independence' that we admire in the Duchess as
'part of a consistent and believable female heroic persona' (Jardine,
cited in Bloom, p. 116). Rather, the Duchess matches what Webster's
source Painter says about her 'naughty life', departing from 'duty and
modesty' (see pp. 95–7):

> In the moment of disobeying her brothers and remarrying (remarrying
> a social inferior, to emphasise that this is 'lust' not 'duty'), the Duchess of
> Malfi asserts her sexual self. In so doing she is metamorphosed from ideal

mirror of virtue ('Let all sweet ladies break their flatt'ring glasses / And dress themselves in her' [I.i.204–5]) into lascivious whore.

(Jardine, p. 121)

Jardine goes on to suggest that close attention to both the legal and practical intricacies of early modern English laws of inheritance will show us how wrong the Duchess is. Following detailed examination of patriarchal power in inheritance, she concludes that

> The Duchess acts out her remarriage and its consequences *as if* her force-fulness as royal heir, dowager of the Dukedom of Amalfi, carrier of a substantial dowry in movable goods (which she and Antonio take legitimately with them when they flee together), gave her *real* power. In this she is proved pathetically wrong.

(Jardine, p. 126)

Citing III.iv.27–33, she suggests that having demonstrated 'looseness' (III.iv.31) by marrying beneath her and without her brothers' consent, she has lost her dower, and is powerless; in effect, not 'Duchess of Malfi still' (IV.ii.141).

Callaghan in 2005 responded similarly to an article looking at the comic treatment of widows in Jacobean theatre, arguing that the frequent feminist account of 'the young merry widow exercising sexual freedom' is 'a cultural fantasy of widowhood', and far from the norm in the early modern period.

Barbara Correll's intriguing article 'Malvolio at Malfi: Managing Desire in Shakespeare and Webster' also puts generic issues to the fore, starting with the possibility that Webster might, during his time at the Middle Temple (see p. 90), have attended the performance of *Twelfth Night* there on 2 February 1602. Did the idea of a tragic Antonio, and perhaps for Bosola, germinate from the rejected comic steward in Shakespeare's comedy? Correll uses this speculation to consider not just the important role of stewards in early modern society, but also the light that such thinking can throw on the Duchess's reaction to her two brothers and her two more lowly but nonetheless upwardly mobile household servants.

With other recent essays dealing with, among other topics, 'the use of the discourses of anatomy and medical science whose proximity to surveillance, rape and torture are analyzed repeatedly'

(Callaghan, 'State of the Art', p. 70), there is a sinister quality to the new critical discourse:

> Precisely those qualities that gave rise to critical derision of Webster as a sensationalist earlier in the twentieth century – highly sexualized violence, cruelty, depravity and the misuse of political power – are in the new millennium understood to be Webster's prescient vision of the parlous fragility of love and innocence. ... The critical ground has shifted decisively [to] an assurance not only that the themes and preoccupations of *Duchess* resonate profoundly with the twenty-first century present, but also that Webster demonstrates an incisive dramaturgical and political vision.
>
> (Callaghan, 'State of the Art', p. 66)

Theatrical and screen criticism

Thomas Middleton, William Rowley, and Orazio Busino are the earliest known critics of *The Duchess of Malfi* (see p. 3) and criticism of performance has existed throughout the play's subsequent stage life, reflecting not just the current literary opinion of the day, but also responding to the interpretation and interaction of actors – what we might call their creative criticism. Latterly, that creative criticism has extended to designers, directors, and a wide range of technical and production staff. Although in the nineteenth century a number of critics condemned stage performance as not living up to the experience of reading Shakespeare, the twentieth and twenty-first centuries have come to see value in investigating the plays as, for us as for Webster, scripts to be realized collaboratively in the theatre or on screen.

John Russell Brown, a pioneer of serious critical study of Shakespeare in performance, is alert to performative alternatives in the Introduction to his Revels Student Edition of *The Duchess of Malfi* (pp. 22–9). The first substantial stage history is David Carnegie's Theatrical Introduction in *The Works of John Webster*, vol. 1, which concludes thus:

> Throughout the performance history of *The Duchess of Malfi* audiences have been moved to pity and admiration by the Duchess, even in the truncated nineteenth-century versions. Difficulties have lain elsewhere, especially with longueurs in Act V. The most successful twentieth-century productions, however, have not been those that have cut heavily or relied on an overwhelming evocation of atmosphere through design or startling

modernity. Rather, they have trusted the playwright, demonstrated the centrality of Bosola as well as the Duchess to the moral focus of the play, and elucidated the theatrical power of the complex interplay of character, structure, and theme.

(Carnegie, p. 442)

Most editions now include attention to the theatrical and performative aspects of the play, and one, Kathleen McLuskie and Jennifer Uglow's edition in the Plays in Performance series, has its Introduction and commentary notes entirely devoted to how the play has been performed in the past.

Richard Allen Cave's short book *The White Devil and The Duchess of Malfi*, in the Text and Performance series, usefully combines a first half of traditional literary analysis of language, character, style, and themes with a second half that looks in detail at four professional production, two of them being Peter Gill's 1971 'Brechtian' production at the Royal Court Theatre, the other the 1985 Philip Prowse production (see pp. 111–13).

Webster is fascinated by the ways conscience manifests itself in the psyche and the ways minds free themselves from the burden of guilt. This is not to argue that he is an aridly moralistic dramatist. He also delights in the arts of the theatre – acting, mime, music, spectacle – and exploits them richly, but to a distinctive purpose. Always his concern is to make his stage-action a metaphor for the inner lives of his characters.

(Cave, pp. 69–70)

In addition, there have been many useful articles and book chapters over recent years dealing with the play as performance (see Further Reading), and Roberta Barker's 'The Duchess High and Low: A Performance History of *The Duchess of Malfi*' usefully brings the record into the twenty-first century, and also into the age of television and filmed versions.

Screen versions of the play have been very few: the two most significant are the 1972 BBC TV version, and a production staged at the Greenwich Theatre in 2010 specifically so that it could by filmed by Stage on Screen (see pp. 123–8). Scholarly attention to Webster on screen is increasing, and a number of articles are listed under Further Reading.

Further Reading

I   The text and early performances

(i)   Editions

Reliable one-volume editions of the play, with scholarly introductions, annotations and textual collations, include those by John Russell Brown (Revels Plays, 2nd edition; Manchester and New York: Manchester University Press, 2009; and Revels Student Editions, 1997); Leah Marcus (Arden Early Modern Drama; London: Methuen Drama, 2009); Elizabeth Brennan (New Mermaids; London: Ernest Benn, 1964; 4th edition Brian Gibbons; London: Methuen Drama, 2009); and René Weis (*The Duchess of Malfi and Other Plays*, Oxford World's Classics; Oxford: Oxford University Press, 1996). The standard critical edition is *The Works of John Webster*, Vol. 1, ed. David Gunby, David Carnegie, and Antony Hammond (Cambridge: Cambridge University Press, 1995). Quotations and references in this *Handbook* are taken from Brown's Revels Student Edition.

(ii)   Theatre history and practice

Authority for the factual information in Chapter 1 will be found in the following, and in the editions cited above.

David Carnegie, 'Theatrical Introduction' to *The Duchess of Malfi* in *Works of John Webster*, Vol. 1, pp. 411–28, a detailed account of the actors, eyewitnesses, and other evidence about the first productions of the play.
Andrew Gurr, *The Shakespearean Stage*, 4th edition (Cambridge: Cambridge University Press, 2009), a thoroughly responsible account of what is known about the theatrical conditions in which Elizabethan and Jacobean plays were first performed.

II   General studies

Harold Bloom, *John Webster's 'The Duchess of Malfi'*, Modern Critical Interpretations (New York: Chelsea House, 1987). This collection includes several major contributions to Webster criticism, but unfortunately has deleted the footnotes that appeared when the essays were originally published.

Rupert Brooke, *John Webster and the Elizabethan Drama* (New York: John Lane, 1916). An important early study that makes a case for Webster as a major playwright.

M. C. Bradbrook, *John Webster: Citizen and Dramatist* (London: Weidenfeld and Nicolson, 1980). The first book-length study to take account of new discoveries about Webster's birth and London connections. Has a chapter on *The Duchess of Malfi*. Always lively, and usually trustworthy.

Dympna Callaghan (ed.), *New Casebooks: The Duchess of Malfi: John Webster*, (Basingstoke: Macmillan/New York: St Martin's Press, 2000). A valuable collection of essays foregrounding gender and feminist critiques.

Charles Forker, *Skull Beneath the Skin: The Achievement of John Webster* (Carbondale and Edwardsville: Southern Illinois University Press, 1986). An exhaustive and reliable study of Webster's life and writing. Chapter 7 (pp. 296–369) is devoted to *The Duchess of Malfi*.

David Gunby, 'Webster, John (1578x80–1638?)', in the *Oxford Dictionary of National Biography* (Oxford: Oxford University Press, 2004–13), online at http://www.oxforddnb.com/view/article/28943 (subscription required, accessed 14 April 2014). Also available in print version, ed. H. C. G. Mathew and B. H. Harrison, 60 vols (Oxford: Oxford University Press, 2004). An authoritative brief biography and account of Webster's work and critical reputation.

G. K. and S. K. Hunter (eds.), *John Webster* (Harmondsworth: Penguin, 1969). A valuable collection of essays, including consideration of productions.

Christina Luckyj (ed.), *The Duchess of Malfi: A Critical Guide* (London and New York: Continuum, 2011). A casebook of significant new articles, and surveys of both critical reception and performance, with a substantial listing of print, audio, screen, online, and other resources for study and teaching of the play.

Don D. Moore (ed.), *Webster: The Critical Heritage* (London, Boston, and Henley: Routledge and Kegan Paul, 1981). A compilation, with brief introductions, of all major critical voices from 1617 to the end of the nineteenth century.

Brian Morris (ed.), *John Webster* (London: Benn, 1970). This collection of essays includes several on *The Duchess of Malfi*, theatrical as well as critical.

Norman Rabkin (ed.), *Twentieth Century Interpretations of The Duchess of Malfi: A Collection of Critical Essays* (Englewood Cliffs, NJ: Prentice-Hall, 1968).

A now somewhat dated but nonetheless useful collection of essays, including Inga-Stina Ekeblad's influential article, 'The "Impure Art" of John Webster'.

Margaret Loftus Ranald, *John Webster*, Twayne's English Authors (Boston: Twayne, 1989). A concise guide to Webster's life and work, with a short critical chapter on each play that includes a brief summation of performance history.

Rowland Wymer, *Webster and Ford*, English Dramatists (Basingstoke: Palgrave Macmillan, 1995). Introduced with brief but cogent historical and critical material, the chapter on *The Duchess of Malfi* is alert to both performative and theoretical views of the play.

III   Sources

William Painter, *The Palace of Pleasure* [1567], 3 vols (New York: Dover, 1966). A modern edition of Webster's primary source, Painter's translation from the French of François de Belleforest's *Histoire Tragicques* (1565), itself based on Matteo Bandello's Italian *Novelle* (1554–73).

Sir Philip Sidney, *The Countess of Pembroke's Arcadia*, ed. Albert Feuillerat (Cambridge: Cambridge University Press, 1912).

(Note: for discussion of other sources, see Gunby et al., *Works of John Webster*, Sources; Boklund; Albert H. Tricomi, 'The Severed Hand in Webster's *Duchess of Malfi*', *Studies in English Literature, 1500–1900* 44, pp. 347–58; and, challenging Tricomi, Brett D. Hirsch, 'Werewolves and Severed Hands: Webster's *The Duchess of Malfi* and Heywood and Brome's *The Witches of Lancashire*', *Notes and Queries* 53 (2006), pp. 92–4.)

IV   The play in production and performance

Roberta Barker, '"Another Voyage": Death as Social Performance in the Major Tragedies of John Webster', *Early Theatre* 8.2 (2005), 35–56. Principally a comparison of Flamineo in *The White Devil* with Bosola as shape-shifters whose metatheatrical references to their own deaths may invoke a spectator identification in the theatre that is difficult to perceive when simply reading the play.

Roberta Barker, 'An Actor in the Main of All: Individual and Relational Selves in *The Duchess of Malfi*', in *Early Modern Tragedy, Gender, and Performance,1984–2000: The Destined Livery* (New York: Palgrave, 2007). Considers the relationship between the Duchess and the male characters in two recent professional productions.

Roberta Barker, 'The Duchess High and Low: A Performance History of *The Duchess of Malfi*', in Luckyj, *Critical Guide*, pp. 42–65. A useful reconsideration and updating of Carnegie, 'Theatrical Introduction', especially in its attention to recent stage and screen versions.

John Russell Brown, 'Techniques of Restoration' in *Shakespearean Illuminations: Essays in Honour of Marvin Rosenberg*, ed. Jay L. Halio and Hugh Richmond (Newark, DE and London: University of Delaware Press/Associated University Presses, 1998), pp. 317–35. A valuable close examination of two contrasting professional productions of *The Duchess of Malfi* in London in the 1990s.

David Carnegie, 'Theatrical Introduction' to *The Duchess of Malfi* in *Works of John Webster*, Vol. 1, pp. 408–49. A detailed examination of the conditions of performance of the original productions 1614–23, and a consideration of both Webster's stagecraft and performance history to 1990.

Richard Allen Cave, *The White Devil and The Duchess of Malfi: Text and Performance* (Basingstoke and London: Macmillan Education, 1988). A handbook that in the first half offers a literary critique of language, imagery, character, and action; in the second half each play is closely investigated in two contrasting productions (for *The Duchess of Malfi*, Peter Gill's Brechtian 1971 production at the Royal Court Theatre in London, and Philip Prowse's design-heavy production for the National Theatre of Great Britain in 1985).

Kathleen McLuskie and Jennifer Uglow (eds.), *The Duchess of Malfi* by John Webster, Plays in Performance (Bristol: Bristol Classical Press, 1989). An edition of the complete play with introduction and notes concentrating on historical stage interpretations and business.

Benedict Nightingale, 'Dramatic Restorers at Work', *The Times* (29 December 1995). A feature on the then forthcoming Cheek by Jowl production in 1995, including extracts from an interview with the director.

Keith Sturgess, '"A Perspective that shows us Hell": *The Duchess of Malfi* at the Blackfriars', in *Jacobean Private Theatre*, by Keith Sturgess (London and New York: Routledge and Kegan Paul, 1987). A lively and generally astute examination of the stagecraft Webster has written into performance for its first production at the Blackfriars.

V Screen and audio versions

Because recordings are liable to be offered in varying formats with new reference numbers, only titles and directors' names are given here together with the original release date; from this information, the latest and most convenient reissue can be identified.

(i) Screen versions

The Duchess of Malfi, directed by James McTaggart, 1972 (BBC), 1975 (PBS).

The Duchess of Malfi, directed by Elizabeth Freestone (stage,) and Chris Cowey (screen), 2010 (Stage on Screen at Greenwich Theatre).

Adaptations

Sweet Smell of Success, directed by Alexander Mackendrick, 1957.

A Question about Hell, written by Kingsley Amis, directed by Claude Whatham 1964 (Granada Television).

Privileged, directed by Michael Hoffman, 1982.

Hotel, directed by Mike Figgis, 2001.

Quietus, directed by Peter Huby, 2002 (not yet released; but see Wymer's 'Huby's *Quietus*').

Revenge for the Duchess of Malfi, directed by Kyle McDonald and Philip Borg, 2010 (10 min. film http://www.dailymotion.com/video/xd679z_revenge-for-the-duchess-of-malfi_shortfilms# accessed 14 April 2014).

(ii) Audio versions

The Duchess of Malfi, directed by R. D. Smith (BBC broadcast 1954; cassettes released 1980).

The Duchess of Malfi, directed by Howard Sackler (Caedmon, 1968; now HarperCollins Audio).

The Duchess of Malfi, directed by Alison Hindon (BBC broadcast 1992; online at http://www.mixcloud.com/nazarethgayle/duchess-of-malfi-john-webster/ accessed 14 April 2014).

The Duchess of Malfi, directed by Roy McMillan (BBC broadcast 2008; not currently available).

'O, Let Us Howl', sung by Julianne Baird (soprano) and Ronn McFarlane (lute), *The English Lute Song* (Dorian recordings, 1988; DOR-90109). CD.

(iii) Articles on screen versions

Pascale Aebischer, 'Shakespearean Heritage and the Preposterous "Contemporary Jacobean" Film: Mike Figgis's *Hotel*', *Shakespeare Quarterly* 60 (2009), pp. 279–303. A detailed critique of *Hotel* as a radical adaptation of Webster that finally fails to transcend the ideological targets of its criticism.

Pascale Aebischer, 'Early Modern Performance and Digital Media: Remediation and the Evolving Archival Canon', in *Beyond Shakespeare: Screening Early Modern Drama* (Cambridge: Cambridge University Press, 2013). A valuable examination of the role of YouTube and social media in reconstituting such ephemeral events as the Punchdrunk theatre company's secretive production for English National Opera, and screen versions not otherwise publicly available, including the 1972 BBC-TV version, McDonald and Borg's *Revenge for the Duchess of Malfi*, and Hubey's *Quietus*.

Tim Band, 'Review of John Webster's *The Duchess of Malfi* and Ben Jonson's *Volpone* (directed by Elizabeth Freestone) at Greenwich Theatre, 10 April 2010', *Shakespeare* 7 (2011), pp. 86–91. A brief review of the stage production on which the 2010 Stage on Screen video is based.

David Carnegie 'Webster's *The Duchess of Malfi* on TV', *Shakespeare on Film Newsletter* 12 (December 1987), pp. 1–2. A brief critique demonstrating the extent of unusually non-realist, formalist television technique in the 1972 BBC screen version.

Susanne Greenhalgh, 'The Jacobeans on Television: *The Duchess of Malfi* and *'Tis Pity She's a Whore* at Chastleton House, *Shakespeare Bulletin* 29 (2011), pp. 573–89. A more extended article than Carnegie's on the same BBC TV version, concentrating on the visual use of the real house used for the shoot.

G. K. and S. K. Hunter, 'Modern Productions and Adaptations', in Hunter, pp. 305–11. Stage coverage ends in 1945, but a brief account of Amis's TV adaptation 'A Question about Hell' is added.

Rowland Wymer, 'The Duchess of Malfi on Film: Peter Huby's *Quietus*', in *Reinventing the Renaissance: Shakespeare and his Contemporaries in Adaptation and Performance*, ed. Sarah Brown, Robert Lublin, and Lynsey McCulloch (Basingstoke: Palgrave Macmillan, 2013). Includes a detailed account of actual and intended screen versions, and is a useful complement to Aebischer's article on Figgis's *Hotel*.

VI   Critical assessments

Kate Aughterson, *Webster: The Tragedies* (Basingstoke: Palgrave, 2001).

Ralph Berry, *The Art of John Webster* (Oxford: Clarendon Press, 1972).

Catherine Belsey, 'Emblem and Antithesis in *The Duchess of Malfi*', *Renaissance Drama* n.s. 11 (1980), pp. 115–34; reprinted in Bloom.

Lee Bliss, *The World's Perspective: John Webster and the Jacobean Drama* (New Brunswick, NJ: Rutgers University Press, 1983).

Travis Bogard, *The Tragic Satire of John Webster* (Berkeley: University of California Press, 1955).

Gunnar Bocklund, *The Duchess of Malfi: Sources, Themes, Characters* (Cambridge: Cambridge University Press, 1962).

C. V. Boyer, *The Villain as Hero in Elizabethan Tragedy* (London: Routledge, 1914).

Dympna Callaghan, *Woman and Gender in Renaissance Tragedy: A Study of 'King Lear', 'Othello', 'The Duchess of Malfi', and 'The White Devil'* (Brighton: Harvester, 1989).

Dympna Callaghan, 'The State of the Art: Critical Approaches 2000–08', in Luckyj, *Critical Guide*.

Lord David Cecil, *Poets and Storytellers* (London: Constable, 1949); excerpt reprinted in Hunter.

Barbara Correll, 'Malvolio at Malfi: Managing Desire in Shakespeare and Webster', *Shakespeare Quarterly* 58 (2007), pp. 65–92.

Christy Desmet, '"Neither Maid, Widow, nor Wife": Rhetoric of the Woman Controversy in *The Duchess of Malfi*', in *In Another Country: Feminist Perspectives on Renaissance Drama*, ed. Dorothea Kehler and Susan Baker (London: Scarecrow, 1991); reprinted in Callaghan, *New Casebooks*.

Bettie Anne Doebler, 'Continuity in the Art of Dying: *The Duchess of Malfi*', *Comparative Drama* 14 (1980), pp. 203–15; reprinted in Bloom.

W. A. Edwards, 'John Webster', *Scrutiny* 2 (1933), pp. 12–23.

Inga-Stina Ekeblad, 'The "Impure Art" of John Webster', *Review of English Studies* n.s. 9 (1958), pp. 253–67; reprinted in Rabkin, and in Hunter.

T. S. Eliot, 'Four Elizabethan Dramatists', in *Selected Essays* (London: Faber and Faber, 1932).

Una Ellis-Fermor, *The Jacobean Drama* (London: Methuen, 1936).

Dana Goldberg, *Between Worlds: A Study of the Plays of John Webster* (Waterloo, Ontario: Wilfred Laurier University Press, 1987).

David Gunby, 'The Critical Backstory', in Luckyj, *Critical Guide*.

David Gunby, '*The Duchess of Malfi*: A Theological Approach', in *John Webster*, ed. Brian Morris (London: Benn, 1970).

David Gunby, '"Strong Commanding Art": The Structure of *The White Devil*, *The Duchess of Malfi*, and *The Devil's Law-Case*', in *Words that Count: Essays in Early Modern Authorship in Honor of MacDonald P. Jackson*, ed. Brian Boyd (Newark, DE: University of Delaware Press, 2004).

Ian Jack, 'The Case of John Webster', *Scrutiny* 16 (1949), pp. 38–43; reprinted in Hunter.

Ken Jackson, '"Twin Shows of Madness": John Webster's Stage Management of Bethlem in *The Duchess of Malfi*', in *Separate Theaters: Bethlem ('Bedlam') Hospital and the Shakespearean Stage* (Newark, DE: University of Delaware Press, 2005).

Theodora Jankowski, 'Defining/Confining the Duchess: Negotiating the Female Body in John Webster's *The Duchess of Malfi*', *Studies in Philology* 87 (1990), pp. 221–45; reprinted in Callaghan, *New Casebooks*.

Lisa Jardine, '*The Duchess of Malfi*: A Case Study in the Literary Representation of Women', in *Teaching the Text*, ed. Suzanne Kappeler and Norman Bryson (London: Routledge and Kegan Paul, 1983); reprinted in Bloom.

Charles Lamb, *Specimens of English Dramatists* (London: Longman, 1808); excerpt reprinted in Moore.

Clifford Leech, *Webster: The Duchess of Malfi* (London: Edward Arnold, 1963).

Hester Lees-Jeffries, 'The Public Fountain: Elizabethan Politics and the Humanist Tradition', in *England's Helicon: Fountains in Early Modern Literature and Culture* (New York: Oxford University Press, 2007).

Jeremy Lopez, 'Managing Asides', in *Theatrical Conventions and Audience Response in Early Modern Drama* (Cambridge: Cambridge University Press, 2003).

Christina Luckyj, *A Winter's Snake: Dramatic Form in the Tragedies of John Webster* (Athens, GA: University of Georgia Press, 1989).

Peter B. Murray, *A Study of John Webster* (The Hague: Mouton, 1969).

Michael Neill, *Issues of Death: Mortality and Identity in English Renaissance Tragedy* (Oxford: Clarendon Press, 1998).

Robert Ornstein, *The Moral Vision of Jacobean Tragedy* (Madison: University of Wisconsin Press, 1960).

Jacqueline Pearson, *Tragedy and Tragicomedy in the Plays of John Webster* (Manchester: Manchester University Press, 1980).

Joyce E. Peterson, *'Curs'd Example': 'The Duchess of Malfi' and Commonweal Tragedy* (Columbia: University of Missouri Press, 1978).

Hereward T. Price, 'The Function of Imagery in Webster', *PMLA* 70 (1955), pp. 717–39; reprinted in Hunter.

Mary Beth Rose, *The Expense of Spirit: Love and Sexuality in English Renaissance Drama* (Ithaca: Cornell University Press, 1988).

L. G. Salingar, 'Tourneur and the Tragedy of Revenge', in *The Pelican Guide to English Literature*, vol. 2, revised edition, ed. Boris Ford (Harmondsworth: Penguin, 1960).

Charlotte Spivack, '*The Duchess of Malfi*: A Fearful Madness', *Journal of Women's Studies in Literature* 2 (1979), pp. 122–32.

Wendy Wall, 'Just a Spoonful of Sugar: Syrup and Domesticity in Early Modern England', *Modern Philology* 104 (2006), pp. 149–72.

Frank Whigham, 'Sexual and Social Mobility in *The Duchess of Malfi*', *PMLA* 100 (1985), pp. 167–86; reprinted in Callaghan, *New Casebooks*.

Index